THE REVELATION OF GOD'S SONS

DISCOVER THE PURPOSE OF YOUR LIFE

This book is also available in eBook version.

ISBN: 978-2-95-576564-7
© Published by Pascal Malonda, Paris, 2017

Original title: LA RÉVÉLATION DES FILS DE DIEU
Translation: Alex Richards and Marie Verpilleux
All rights reserved for all countries.

THE REVELATION OF GOD'S SONS

DISCOVER THE PURPOSE OF YOUR LIFE

PASCAL MALONDA

This book is dedicated to God,
the initiator and inspiration of this project,
as well as to my parents.
You are forever my heroes.

"For the creation waits in eager expectation for the children of God to be revealed."

(Romans 8: v. 19)

Introduction

The story of this book begins on July 10, 2013. At that time, I had no idea about how a significant turning point in my life this would be. That day, while driving my car, like most mornings, I was immersed in my thoughts. While all sorts of meaningless ideas and images were parading in my mind, my attention was caught by the thought of eternity. At that very moment, I could see myself in heaven, holding in my hands all the deeds I had done, while on earth. There was a man standing in front of me and I understood right away that He was Jesus. He warmly greeted me and said: "Enter into the joy of your master, good and faithful servant"[1]. Upon hearing those words, an inner joy filled my heart, for I understood that the gates of eternity were wide open for me. A few steps from where we were standing, there was an altar from which huge flames were burning. Jesus then took my works and threw them into the fire. I could hear the crackling as they were being consumed. Some black smoke arose, and then nothing. They had just been set ablaze, like straw. Surprised by the scene, I turned to Jesus and asked: "Where are the rewards for all I have done? Have I not gained anything?" He pointed at a gigantic screen that appeared in front of me and said: "Look,

---

1. 1. Matthew 25:21.

this the life you could have lived". Images scrolled before my eyes at high speed, and I couldn't understand what it was all about. However, from that day, a deep conviction was anchored in my heart: the life I should have had was immeasurably better than the one I did have. Yet, to me, I had experienced many beautiful things. How could I have had a better life than this one?

Three days later, I arrived at the Las Vegas airport for a three-week vacation. On Sunday, I went to a church located fifteen minutes away from downtown, the International Church of Las Vegas. The pastor Paul Goulet was teaching that day on the importance of growing spiritually, on expanding one's "inner being". During his teaching, he picked the following example to illustrate his point: "Imagine for a moment that you are in heaven. You are standing in front of Jesus and He tells you: "Enter into the joy of your master, good and faithful servant". You give Him your works. He puts them into the fire. The fire burns them all and you realize you are left with nothing in return! Sure, you are saved, but you missed the life God had planned for you." As he went on speaking, I realized that he was describing word for word what I had experienced a few days before. Although we were about 800 people in that building, this message was directly addressed to me. It was not a figment of my imagination, it was indeed a message that God wanted to pass me. From then on, I was left with no excuse. I did not know which life God had planned for me, but one thing was sure: I could no longer bury my head in the sand. I simply had to discover why was I born and what He had planned for my life.

Understanding Destiny led me to discover and grasp the meaning of life and the reason for our existence on earth. It brought me to grasp what our place in this wide universe is and the link that unites Man to God. This research led me to devour books, articles and journals dealing with the topic, attend seminars and conferences, discuss with men and women who were also in a quest for the purpose of their life, and meet people who had completed significant things, because they had understood the reason why they were there; and finally enter my own destiny.

This allowed me to understand who I was and now enables me to help you discover who you are. This understanding is possible only when you realize that God is at the core of life. The denial of His existence has developed a vacuum in men's hearts and all their attempts to fill that void on their own have resulted into deep dissatisfaction and extreme excesses in our world. Our world is anesthetized by the darkness that slowly settles down, but men do not pay attention. They are blinded by their lives' artificial light and would rather convince themselves that all is well, as long as their daily reality is not shaken by the tragedies seen in the daily news. But over 2,000 years ago, three wise men saw another light. It was a star, shining in the sky.

They followed it and it led them to Jesus, the Son of God, the Savior of the world, the One that the Holy Scriptures call the Morning Star. In an era where God's voice becomes inaudible to humans, where darkness overtakes our societies, He desires to make stars emerge, His sons and daughters, so they bring light and truth where they are. While clash of cultures, relationships between peoples and mistrust towards politicians are stronger than ever, the time has come for the sons and daughters of God to be revealed.

This book is neither eschatological nor religious because those discourses rarely bring solutions. It rather aims at breaking with the religious spirit and put God back at the center of Creation. The religious spirit defines itself as an attempt by Man to draw closer to God, by creating a set of rules and precepts, rooted in human traditions and understandings, or as the fact for a believer to be convinced that obedience to rules would lead them closer to God.

In both cases, this way of thinking has resulted in making the "relationship" between the believer and God monotonous, guilt-inducing and frustrating. No matter what one does, they can never find fulfillment if they do not reconnect with the Source of life, which will lead to a better understanding of the purpose of their life.

This book is divided into four parts:

- The first part "The consequences of a world without God", draws up an observation of the current situation within our modern societies and how we got there.

- The second part "Between God and Man", takes us back to the origins of Creation and to God's plan for Man.

- The third part "Begin living a victorious life" reminds us that those who have chosen to really walk with God will be able to live a victorious life, not one exempt from trials and difficulties but one in which trials and difficulties make them stronger.

- The fourth part "Destiny", allows us to grasp the purpose of our presence on earth and understand how God has chosen His people to represent Him.

FIRST PART

The consequences of a world without God

Chapter 1
The thought of God from Antiquity to our days

1 – Little science may take oneaway from God; much science brings one back[1]

Since the dawn of time, Man has never stopped wondering what his place was in the universe. The complexity and immensity of the heavens awaken in him a multitude of questions, which he still cannot answer. These questions lead him to the very depths of his soul, in the infinity of his thoughts, reasoning and imagination. He asks himself: "Ultimately, what is my role on earth? What is the purpose and the meaning of my life?" The renowned biologist Thomas Huxley once said:

> The supreme question for
> mankind, the original problem
> that is of greater concern to us

---

1. Quote from Louis Pasteur, famous French scientist (1822-1895).

than any other, is the definition of the place that man occupies in nature and his relationships with most things. Where do we come from? What are the boundaries of our power over nature and that of nature over us? **What is our purpose and destiny?**[2]

Scientific progress has enabled to establish that the universe is governed by a mathematical language that obeys laws which, joining, allow it to exist. The Earth is governed by a set of physical and natural laws and we now know that human life is possible only because it obeys these laws. The spirit of Man is also subject to invisible laws, embedded in his consciousness. Contrary to nature, which is voluntarily submissive, Man has the option of choosing what he considers good or bad for his life and each decision will shape it. The complexity of the universe and life on earth is such that it becomes increasingly more difficult for the most persistent atheist scientists to defend that the Earth and the entire Solar system are merely a matter of happenstance.

The mathematician Euclid, in his time (300 years B.C.), had already established this observation. He stated: "The laws of nature are nothing else than the mathematical thinking of God"[3]. If Euclid already doubted the absence of God and if today's scientists still haven't managed to

---

2. Thomas Huxley: *Evidence as to Man's Place in Nature*. London, 1863.
3. Igor and Grichka Bogdanov: *La Fin du Hasard, Ed. Grasset, Paris, 2013, p.7 (Coll. « J'ai Lu »)*.

replace God with happenstance, what evidence do nature and the Bible provide to explain a God Creator of all that exists?

- **God is revealed through Creation and the Bible**

Darwinists often blame creationists for believing in God, without evidence but faith. Faith, it is true, is the main element that allows one to grasp the spiritual reality of God. But there is much more than it, if we observe nature, the footprint of its Creator. Theologians have even introduced the metaphor according to which God reveals Himself through "two books": the universal book that is nature, which reveals the hand of the Creator, and the Holy Scriptures[4], that is the Word of God, in other words, the Bible. The Apostle Paul also supports this thesis in the Bible, in the first chapter of the Book of Romans, in which he explains that any man who carefully observes nature will necessarily have to admit that it is the work of God, the Great Creator. He says:

> For since the creation of the world God's invisible qualities - His eternal power and divine nature - have been clearly seen, being understood from what has been made, so that people are without excuse.For although they knew God, they neither glorified Him as God nor gave thanks to Him, but

---

4. Source: http://www.scienceetfoi.com (consulted on December 25, 2015).

their thinking became futile and their foolish hearts were darkened. (Romans 1:20-21)

More recently, in 1936, Albert Einstein came across the same observation, in response to a child asking him if he believed in God. He said: "Anyone who is seriously involved in the pursuit of science becomes convinced that a spirit is manifest in the laws of the Universe, a spirit vastly superior to that of man."[5] While men keep thinking and questioning, it seems that something inexplicable exceeds them. Something beyond their thoughts and reasoning. Something greater in knowledge, strength and power.

Whether Biblical or scientific accounts, the act of creation always seems to be signed by a greater being: God.

- **Science in support of the Bible**

Scientific discoveries in recent years confirm more and more events and facts related in the Bible, and especially the Big Bang as it is described in the Book of Genesis. Among those discoveries, that of physicist and astronomer Robert Woodrow Wilson, who initially thought that the universe had never had a beginning, neither from an explosion nor otherwise. For him the universe was eternal, which questioned the Big Bang theory and whether there has been any creation.

---

5. Igor and Grichka Bogdanov: *Le Visage de Dieu,* Ed. *J'ai LU, Paris, p. 186 (Coll. « J'ai Lu Roman »).*

However, Wilson's research led him to realize later that he was wrong, that there had been a creation of both the universe and space-time. Here is what he declared at a conference:

> The Big Bang corresponds - as told in Genesis - to the creation of everything from nothing: to be consistent with our observations, we must understand that not only was there creation of matter, but there was also creation of space and time. The best data we have is exactly what I would have predicted, had I read nothing else than the five books of Moses, the Psalms and the Bible. The Big Bang was a moment of sudden creations out of nothing.[6]

The fact that modern science confirms that there has been an act of creation and that this act corresponds to the facts chronicled in the Bible is of fundamental importance, because it shows the intervention of a Creator. Through their findings, little by little, scientists restore the beginnings of humanity, the history of Genesis. The famous Bogdanov brothers' ideas are very controversial among the scientific community, especially since their last three books, *The Face of God*, *The Thought of God* and *The End of coincidence* frankly addressed the fact that there is no possible question about the existence of God.

---

6. Extracted from the book *Le Visage de Dieu,* from Igor and Grichka Bogdanov, p. 114 – Conference given at the university of Illinois. Cited by Chuck Colson in *Break Point Big Bang versus Atheist* (September 28, 2006).

However, their perception of the universe is no less interesting. In *The End of coincidence*, they agree with the great scientific discoveries, as they explain the existence of an infinitely greater God. By comparing the moment of creation to a "one in 10,000 billion billion billion billion chance"[7] of coming upon the "right" mathematical value for its outbreak, they reveal an important fact: creation is indeed the result of an intelligent God and certainly not a matter of chance.

2 – God in Western culture

The depiction of God in Western culture has changed a lot over the past centuries. In France for example, from 1789 to the present day, the nation has gradually moved away from the thought of God, making it today one of the leading atheist countries in Europe.

- **France and the fall of Christianity**

History shows us that Christianity has for a long time influenced the French society, as evidenced by many of our laws inspired by Christianity, our Gregorian calendar and even the organization of the cities and villages, in which the church is located at the center.

Today, these same churches are empty and fill up on rare occasions like birth celebrations, weddings and... funerals. Even the celebration of Christmas, symbol of the birth of Christ and integral part of the French history and culture,

---

7. Igor and Grichka Bogdanov: *Le Visage de Dieu*, p. 19.

is more and more despised. There are several reasons behind this: the religious spirit, characterized by purely human dogma and rules, the absence of the Holy Spirit[8], the lack of life, love and warmth, the scandals that plague the Roman Catholic Church, disappointments, the sectarian aberrations and the religious wars among the Christian communities themselves, all have divided the followers.

The laws of secularization also have influenced the school system, by redefining the role of God in education and by voluntarily putting Him aside. What initially appeared to be a good idea, based on republican universality, eventually led to an almost atheist society, that considered the theory of evolution of Charles Darwin as the absolute truth, preferring it to any idea of a God and Creator.

In the light of this information, it thus seems logical that this notion of a life without God has finally settled and taken root in people's mind, particularly among the young, who have grown and evolved in an unbelieving world. Indeed, a recent article written by the journalist Clément Solym considered that "two thirds of young people do not believe in God"[9]. All this raises many existential questions, such as: "How does one believe there could be life after death, when not believing in God?" and "What's the purpose of living, if it is to end up in nothingness?" If it provokes thinking for some and denying for others, death and "void" no longer trigger fear, they are simply seen as natural life events which cannot be changed. Besides, the collective unconsciousness believes that "We all are on our way to paradise", to quote the famous Michel Polnareff

---

8. See chapter 5 for further explanations on the person of the Holy Spirit.
9. Clement Solym, on the ActuaLitté website: https://www.actualitte.com/article/monde-edition/deux-tiers-des-jeunes-ne-croient-pas-en-dieu/11232 (consulted on March 15, 2016).

track. This tune, which has become a leitmotiv, is a good illustration of the fact that the doors of paradise, if there is any, will be wide open to all.

This belief is inherited from Catholicism that, in the Middle Ages, taught its followers the notion of purgatory. According to this theory, there is a place in which people who do not have access to heaven will be given a second chance, by waiting in an intermediary place, until their sins are forgiven. This idea suggests that there might be a second chance after physical death. Even if this thinking predominates in the traditional church, it is inconsistent with the teachings of the Bible. Indeed, the Bible is clear about this: "Just as people are destined to die once, and face judgment afterwards." (Hebrews 9:27).

- **France and the humanist thought**

The humanist thought, born during the Renaissance, has largely contributed to move man away from God. It places man at the center and above all things. Man has become his own God. The humanist thought considers man as intellectually able to cope alone and to support himself. This change of mentality has consequently contributed to a shift, in which priorities are now focused on man himself.

- **France and consumerism**

The "Thirty Glorious Years" have fostered a boom in the economy, jobs, housing, infrastructures and technological progress. That time has enabled the emergence of the middle class which, thanks to access to bank credit, could greatly improve its standard of living, by becoming the owner of a house, a car and all the necessary comfort. In 1982, President François Mitterrand introduced the fifth week of paid leave. Therefore, French families could go on vacation every year and, to quote Voltaire, they could finally say that "all is for the best in the best of all worlds." But what is revealing of human nature here is that with the improvement of the standard of living, came the sweet illusion that goods and material comfort could suffice to make one happy and fill the soul.

In the Bible, King Salomon, described as the wisest man the Earth has ever known and the richest in his day, also experienced the same thing. He also thought at one point that labor and material goods could bring happiness. Yet, after having everything he desired, he said:

> I denied myself nothing my eyes desired; I refused my heart no pleasure. My heart took delight in all my labor, and this was the reward for all my toil. Yet when I surveyed all that my hands had done and what I had toiled to achieve, everything was meaningless, a chasing after the wind; nothing was gained under the sun. (Ecclesiastes 2:10-11)

His quest for happiness led him to acquire everything he wanted, with no restrictions, but his final statement was: "everything was meaningless, a chasing of the wind". His wealth must have procured some happiness, but it was short-lived and never enough to fill his heart. This reminds us that yesterday, just like today, the final analysis is always the same: material goods cannot meet the needs of human beings.

Chapter 2
The modern world in crisis?

1 – A world on the edge of a precipice

- **Shaken foundations**

"The world is increasingly getting worse!" This is a thought we all share as we watch the news. The Syrian conflict has internationally impacted the world, on a geopolitical level. The joys and hopes triggered by the Arab Spring and the arrest of several dictators keep dwindling, as the critical state of some countries has worsened. Here and there some voices begin to express regret over the departure of some of these dictators. Italy has no adequate solution to the thousands of migrants who week after week come ashore on its beaches. France and Germany, which thought they were immune to the migratory waves, must also deal with Syrian and Afghan migrants, who are fleeing war and attempting to save their lives. Europe seems completely helpless regarding the sudden influx of refugees. Not to mention the establishment of the Islamic State, the atrocities and the massacres committed by its fighters. And added to all that, the terrorist attacks and threats in Western Europe and elsewhere.

The job market is not spared. Unemployment, which initially mainly affected people with no qualification, now affects everyone, with no exception. When considering the degradation of the labor market, the rise of insecurity and the lowering standard of living, especially among youngsters, many parents are worried about the future of their children, who are the most affected by unemployment and poverty. Holding a diploma and being trained no longer guarantees a stable and decently paid job, not to mention the fate of those who have neither diploma nor training.

As for ecology and weather conditions, the latest news is just as alarming. The Kyoto Protocol's commitment to reduce greenhouse gas emissions is seldom respected. Pollution is so high in some large cities such as Mexico and Beijing, that the health of their residents is at risk. The hole in the ozone layer is getting larger, resulting in an increasing global warming and melting glaciers. In 2015, specialists noted an increase of the Earth's global temperature by 0.8%. Several islands in the Pacific Ocean and in the Indian Ocean are threatened to be submerged by waters and eventually, their disappearance could have unprecedented consequences, in terms of population displacement and humanitarian crisis. The deforestation of the Amazon rainforest, the lungs of the planet, persists despite the warnings of ecological organizations, and the use of pesticides in crop production causes pollution of the soil and groundwater.

In the face of all this, nature itself seems to rebel against the mistreatments it suffers, provoked by the hand of Man. Superlatives are not enough to qualify and describe these new natural disasters.

Recent years were marked by the 2004 tsunami that hit Indonesia and Thailand, Hurricane Katrina in 2005, that struck the U.S. coast close to New Orleans, the volcanic eruption of Eyjafjöll in Iceland in 2010, which paralyzed a major part of the European air traffic during several days. Earthquakes keep reaching higher and higher magnitudes on the Richter scale: the earthquake in 2010 in Haiti with a magnitude of 7 left some 200,000 dead. The one in Japan in 2011, with a magnitude of 8.1, along with the explosive threat of the Fukushima nuclear plant and rather recently, in April 2015, the earthquake in Nepal, with a magnitude of 7.8, are all record figures!

Not to mention the proliferation of epidemics, viruses and diseases such as Alzheimer, Parkinson and cancers that affect us all, our loved ones near and far. Even today, the world must still deal with poverty, malnutrition, deprivation of drinking water, education issues, etc. Inequalities are growing, the rich get richer and the poor poorer. The purchasing power of the middle class keeps decreasing, while the cost of living and taxes are getting higher and higher. Retirees who only enjoy the minimum pension as sole resource are not spared. Besides, a new category of workers has emerged in recent years: the working poor. Their salary is so low, compared to the cost of living, that it is insufficient to meet their most basic needs. To survive, some are compelled to go live with relatives or on the street, and are fed by charitable organizations.

- **A depressed France**

    France, the most visited destination in the world, is not just known for its cultural heritage, its museums, the Eiffel Tower and its good wine. For several years now, it is reputed to be one of the countries with the highest consumption of antidepressants in the world.

    The World Health Organization estimates that 5% to 8% of the French population is affected by depression every year, which is about 2 to 3 million individuals[1]. Young people are highly affected by this phenomenon. Depression has considerably increased among those aged 18 to 25, being the first cause of illness and suicide and the third cause of death in France. Experts have noted a sharp increase of risk taking behaviors and drug and alcohol consumption among youngsters. An article in Le Point, published in May 2014, headlined: "Depression, major disease among teenagers". Here is an excerpt from the article:

    > Depression is the number one cause of disease in this age group (10 to 19 years) and suicide is the third cause of mortality. Some studies show that all the individuals with mental problems have noted their first symptoms from the age of 14. According to WHO, if teenagers were treated in time, this could prevent deaths and avoid "lifetime sufferings." The experts of the Organization

---

1. From the following website: http://www.la-depression.org/comprendre-la-depression/la-depression-en-chiffre/ (consulted on December 15, 2015).

wish to remind that adolescence is an important moment in life, for it sets the foundations of a healthy adult life. In addition, WHO notes that the three main causes of death among adolescents in the world are: "road accidents, AIDS and suicide." In 2012, 1.3 million teenagers died worldwide.[2]

The number of attempted suicides among adolescents continues to increase over the years. It is the third cause of death among teenagers in the world and the second in France. The causes are diverse: degradation of self-esteem, domestic violence, conflicts, lack of opportunities, etc. During this period of life where teenagers build their identity, their problems weigh so heavily that to some, suicide seems to be liberation, the solution to their problems. Unfortunately, no Western country is exempt from this evil destroyer. First world countries see more depressions and suicides than developing countries.

Medical organizations are overwhelmed with depression on the rise. Most of the time, it is the result of emotional injuries, shocks, despondency, sadness, negative stress, anxiety, dark thoughts and the lack of prospects. For those concerned, the diagnosis and treatment are highly complex, because the roots are very deep. This is what some call "the illness of the soul". Depression has become a public health issue in France and in several European countries. A few make the link with not knowing God, combined with not

---

2. From the website of Le Point: http://www.lepoint.fr/sante/la-depression-premiere-maladie-chez-les-adolescents-14-05-2014-1822855_40.phpn (consulted on January 20, 2016).

knowing their identity through God, or why He is calling them. In turning its back on God, mankind has attempted to replace Him with careers, marriage, cars, houses, vacations, leisure, projects and dreams. The pursuit of happiness has multiplied artificial needs but none of them seems to suffice to meet the needs of the soul. All these things are not bad in principle, but they all have a common element: they are fleeting. Fleeting things cannot fill the void in one's heart. It is true that they provide temporary pleasure and satisfaction, which nevertheless tend to shrink shortly, as passion no longer fills their inner void. According to consumer theory, the consumer has unlimited needs (no saturation), while satisfaction decreases every time a consumption unit is purchased. This microeconomics theory illustrates the fact stated previously. It is also one of the "ills" that affect wealthy people. Knowing they can get whatever they want, some no longer have dreams to fulfill. For those who already experienced it, you know money is quite illusory when it comes to providing contentment to the soul. The philosopher Blaise Pascal once made a statement that has become quite famous:

> There was once in man a true happiness of which there now remain in him only; the mark and empty trace, which he in vain tries to fill from all his surroundings, seeking from things absent the help he does not obtain in things present. But these are all inadequate, **because this infinite abyss** can

only **be filled by an infinite and immutable Object, that is to say, only by God Himself.**[3]

The heart of Man being insatiable and tortuous far from God, this quest for pleasure and for always wanting more has ended up pushing our world to the edge of the precipice.

2 – What is the solution?

- **Ineffective state solutions**

Facing this situation, politicians are completely lost and overwhelmed. They're trying to patch up the breaches, but the ship is already beginning to sway. All kinds of ideas, strategies, plans, reorganizations, restructuring of all kinds have been made, but nothing helps. Economic, social, financial, educational, family, legislative models, which have made several countries become leading nations in the world, are breathless and most experts consider that things will go from bad to worse.

The world is sick, but not knowing which disease it suffers from, it has no idea which specialist it should turn to.

In view of this, some voices arise and say: "If God exists, why does He allow all this?" The very same who, earlier, could not care less about whether God existed or not, would blame Him for every illness on earth, whenever their certainties crumble.

---

3. Blaise Pascal – *Souverain bien* 2 (Laf.148, Sel. 181).

The crisis of the modern world is the responsibility of human beings, not God's. We can't blame God after having rejected Him from all the spheres of our lives. But this would not be the first time that Man accuses God. Adam, the first man, started first. When God asked him, in the garden of Eden: "Have you eaten part of the forbidden tree?" He replied, to absolve himself: "The woman whom you put beside me gave me some, and I ate." (Genesis 3:12). In the aftermath of September 11, 2001, New Yorkers flocked to churches. The shock was so appalling that they needed to reconnect with someone higher and greater. Like a crying child seeking refuge in their parents' arms, when injured. But once the emotion is gone, yesterday's resolutions are thrown away and life restarts as if nothing ever happened. Similarly, after the terrible attacks that hit Paris on November 13, 2015, the slogan "Pray for Paris" could be seen all over the place: on walls, canvases, T-shirts and in the media. In difficult times, people tend to lift their eyes towards heaven.

From the top, God sees their suffering. He wants to heal the physical, emotional, psychological and spiritual wounds of the men and women He created in His image. He dreams of His kingdom coming on earth as it is in heaven. His reign breaks every yoke and every chain, brings freedom, spreads peace and joy, reconstructs families, brings solutions, cures diseases and rebuilds nations.

"If only men could look towards me", He thinks. God wants to intervene, but as surprising as it may seem, He cannot use men and women who reject Him to change things. If He did, He would violate the laws and principles that He set Himself. When God created Man, He gave him free will and made him responsible of the Earth. Man is the master of his will, of his choices and of his deeds. It is up to him to invite the Creator to interfere in his business, so that He takes action.

- **What if the solution was in a people's hands? The people of God**

In the past, God revealed Himself to men and women through the prophets, through His son Jesus and through apostles. The Bible says: "many times and in many ways God has once spoken to our ancestors through the prophets. And now, these last days, it is through his Son, that he spoke."[4] (Heb.1:1). The early church has spread the Gospel all over the world and through centuries, several great spiritual waves have made it possible to reveal the existence and the glory of God to the world, making it visible and palpable.

The Pentecostal movement has significantly expanded since its inception in the early 20th century. The reason for this is the importance the followers give to the Bible and the Holy Spirit. The Holy Spirit works in those churches as at the time of the Acts of the Apostles, encouraging sin and repentance, manifesting the gifts of the Holy Spirit and through signs, wonders and healings which reveal the Kingdom of God on earth.

Pastor Tony Cauchi of Revival Library studied the various revivals that occurred throughout the world, based on the research conducted by the theologian J. Edwin Orr. This theology professor has identified six main waves of

---

4. Text from the Semeur version.

revival in the world since Protestant reform[5] until the beginning of the 20th century, each one respectively beginning in 1727, 1792, 1830, 1875, 1882 and 1904. Toni Cauchi wrote: "These progressive revival periods are undeniably the means God has used to thwart the spiritual decline in church and promote a spiritual advancement worldwide."[6] The awakening is characterized by the presence and work of the Holy Spirit that is more and more powerful, visible and palpable. Men and women are so convinced of sin and repentance. The physical, emotional and spiritual healings, as well as signs and miracles are increasingly numerous and extraordinary. The revival penetrates homes, villages and cities. The last great revival began in 1904 and increased in 1906 on Azusa Street, Los Angeles. From this revival, the Pentecostal movement was born, grew over the years and expanded to the whole world through the works of missionaries. It is from that revival that the Pentecostal churches of France were born.

There are today more than 500 million Pentecostal believers in the world and about 900,000 in France. Several signs and prophecies from around the world indicate that God has marked this time and this period to again reveal Himself in a powerful way to the world. Even if it is not relayed by the conventional media, we witness miraculous events obviously initiated by divine intervention, all over

---

5. This is a movement that was initiated by some theologians such as martin Luther, Ulrich Zwingli, Martin Bruce and Jean Calvin. It started at the beginning of the 15th century and this, until the 16th century, to initiate a return to Christianity and also, by extension, a need to consider religion and social life from a different standpoint.
6. From the website of « Revival Library »: http://www.revival-library.org/index.php/pensketches-menu/historical-revivals/general-overview-of-revivals (consulted on December 29, 2015).

the world: testimonies from people who were dead and came back to life, cancers miraculously healed, depressive people who found inner peace, drug addicts who are freed of their addictions, broken homes that are restored, men and women who find a life purpose, etc. Pastor Ché Ahn, from Harvest Church in Pasadena, says the following in his book When Heaven Comes Down:

> From all over the world, I receive testimonials of the power of God bringing dead people back to life. Rolland and Heidi Baker, founders of Iris Ministries, have seen more than 80 people resurrecting from the dead in their ministry in Africa, Europe and Asia.[7]

The Evangelist Daniel Kolenda, who is involved in huge crusades of evangelization in Africa[8] that bring together hundreds of thousands of people, regularly sees miracles during his meetings: the blind recover vision, deaf people hear again, mute people talk, paralyzed ones walk, malformations disappear, possessed individuals get delivered, insane people get back on track. God wants to extend this throughout the world so that people realize that this is all real. He wants to stretch out His hand all over Europe so they see and believe, too. For this, He has chosen to work with ordinary people who carry an extraordinary power: the power of the Holy Spirit. God is raising a generation of

---

7. Ché Ahn: *When Heaven comes down: Experiencing God's glory in your life*, p.67.
8. Evangelization crusades "Africa shall be saved", with Daniel Kolenda and Reinhard Bonnke.

men and women who have strong desire to see change in their families, friends, neighbors and nation. It begins with His people: those who have chosen to follow Him, arousing a greater thirst for Him and His presence, deep inside them. To achieve this, He lights up a flame within their hearts and places therein love for people, a burden for the salvation of souls and for this dying world. His desire remains the same: heal the broken hearted, set the captives free, rescue the ones in need, in other words: spread His love all over the world. God is sovereign, He could act on His own but He has chosen to work with His church. When I talk about the church, I am not talking about names, buildings or physical places, but I am rather referring to men and women, young and not so young, touched by the love of God, who desire to share this love around them. Workers, students, entrepreneurs, artists and retirees. How did this relationship between the Creator and Man come to an end? This is what we are about to consider in the second part.

SECOND PART

Between God and Man

Chapter 1
The first men and the redemption plan for humanity

While our society is shaken by multiple crises, it is good to go back to the genesis of humanity, in order to remember what God's original plan for Earth and humanity was and thus understand how, eventually, we ended up living in such troubled times.

1 – The creation of the world

- **The physical world**

> In the beginning God created the heavens and the earth. The Earth was formless and empty, darkness was over the surface of the deep, and the Spirit of God was hovering over the waters. And God said, "Let there be light," (Genesis 1:1-3)

God exists from eternity. He has neither beginning nor end. He was, He is and He is to come. The Bible states it. Human life is so small when compared to the eternity of the Creator. Nevertheless, He created Man and it is neither because of a "need", nor because of a "lack", but because He wishes to offer and share what He has. So, God created this wonderful creature called Man, a living being in His image, a work of art. He wants to make this wonderful creature His child, His spiritual relative and share His love and His life.

This is what explains His comments during the Creation of the world: "then God said: "let us make man in our image, in our likeness" (…) God created Man in His image. He created man and woman" (Genesis 1:26-27). Thus, all creation is the result of an inspiration or a representation of its creator. When a sculptor makes a sculpture, he shapes from an idea or an image in his mind. Here, God created Man from Himself, from His image. He was inspired by a perfect model: Himself. Man and woman were created perfect, without any flaw. He gave them His character, His personality, His creativity, His spirit of leadership. The filiation between the Creator and humanity is equivalent to the relationship between a father and his children. A peaceful relationship, founded on love and trust, that builds on. This is very important because it is far from the depiction people have in mind nowadays. It is also diametrically opposed to the image of terror or bogeyman we often see in the collective unconscious or in some religions and beliefs.

"Then the Lord God formed a man from the dust of the ground and breathed into his nostrils the breath of life, and the man became a living being" (Genesis 2:7). Other versions such as Darby's say: "Man became a living soul"[1]. And so, He created man from dust and *breathed a **breath of life** into his nostrils*. He received both an immaterial spirit as well as the physical breath that gave life to his body. God, who is Spirit, created Man in His own image, the spirit of Man is therefore of the same nature as God's. The spirit is the vital part of the human being. It is the headquarters, the reason, the intelligence and the will[2]. He hears the voice of God and communicates with Him, he has access to the spiritual, the supernatural world.

Human beings are tripartite living beings, consisting of a spirit, a soul and a body (fig. 1-A). In the beginning, Man was in communion with God in his soul, his mind and his body. His thoughts, his will and his emotions were in perfect harmony with God. He was living the life God had intended for him.

---

1. Darby version.
2. From the Pasteurweb website: http://www.pasteurweb.org/Etudes/LEtre-Humain/LEtreHumainEspritAmeCorps.htm (consulted on October 15, 2015).

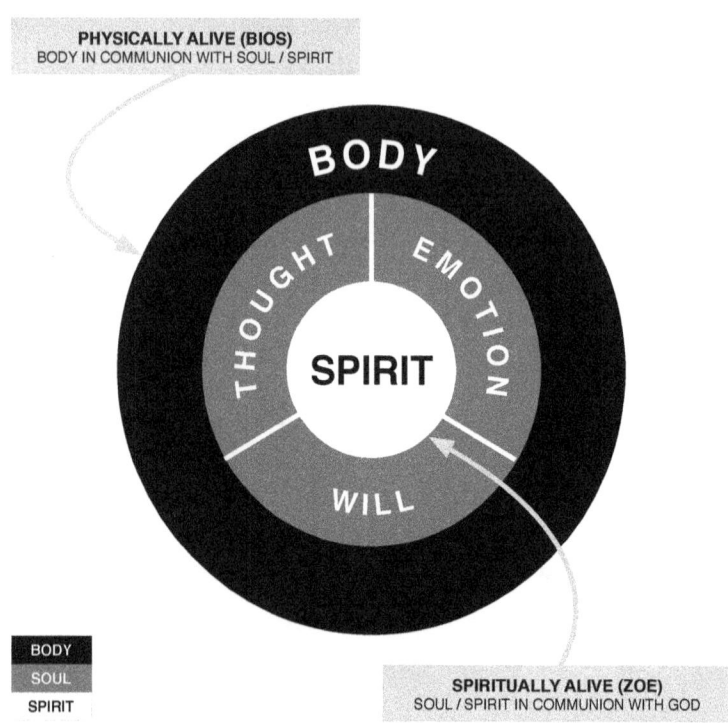

Figure 1 - A4[3]

The spirit does not die, it is immortal. When death occurs, whatever the cause, accidental or natural, the breath of life leaves the body and the spirit goes with God if the individual had chosen to follow Him, or goes to hell otherwise.

The soul is the seat of the thoughts, emotions and will. The dominant thoughts that we feed regularly, undeniably have an effect on our character and personality, as this proverb from King Solomon reminds us: "Because he [Man] is

---

3. Source: Neil T. Anderson, *Victory over darkness*, p. 29.

like the thoughts of his soul" (Proverbs 23:7). The personality of an individual is somehow a reflection of thoughts that dominate them the most. For example, imagine a person who constantly has bad thoughts. After a while, it will negatively affect their mood, character, and thus, personality. This person will tend to have a shady character, see evil everywhere and will be known by others as better to avoid, especially if you plan to spend a pleasant day away from any trace of pessimism.

On the other hand, the person who feeds positive thoughts on a regular basis is generally in good emotional health, seen as cheerful and outgoing. The soul is the link between the mind and the body (Figure 1-A). If we use computer language, it can be said that the soul receives information from the spirit, treats it and makes it intelligible to our consciousness and in some cases, transmits the information to the body. The soul is both the processor and the hard drive. It keeps track of events. It is the center, the heart, the control tower of the entire being. When one's soul is at peace, the entire being is appeased. When your soul is worried, anxiety spreads throughout your body. That is why it is important to feed one's soul with good things. We will discuss this in further detail in the upcoming chapters.

The body is the envelope that enables us to live in this physical world. It is in contact with the material world and sends information to the soul, through all human senses: hearing, smell, touch, sight and taste. We see that the spirit belongs to the spiritual word, the body to the physical world and the soul connects the two.

- **The spiritual world**

We have very little information about the spiritual world, apart from what the Bible says. There are other sources, kept by occult circles, the information often being so obscure that we will stick to the Word of God, because it is the only doctrine on the spiritual world that has authority. The Bible teaches us that there are two worlds: the visible world and the invisible world, in other words the material world and the supernatural or spiritual world.

The heavens were created before the Earth. The book of genesis begins with the following sentence: "In the beginning, God created the **heavens** and the **earth**" (Genesis 1:1). It may seem surprising that the Bible does not say "God created the sky" but rather "God created the heavens". The Apostle Paul explains this plural form in the second book to the Corinthians. Here is what Paul says:

> I know a man in Christ who, fourteen years ago, **was caught up to the third heaven**. Whether it was in the body or out of the body I do not know - God knows. And I know that this man - whether in the body or apart from the body I do not know, but God knows - **was caught up to paradise** and heard inexpressible things, things that no one is permitted to tell. (2 Corinthians 12:2-4)

Many theologians agree that the first sky corresponds to the atmosphere in which we live, and the second sky is the universe, with the stars and planets[4]. The third heaven is the place where the throne of God and angels reside. The throne of God is beyond time and space. It is beyond any human reality[5]. It has neither beginning nor end, it is eternal. This concept is difficult to understand to those who want to assign limits and explanations to everything that surrounds them.

Fallen angels (demons) are found in the second heaven and on earth. The spiritual world consists of the throne of God, celestial beings and angels.

In the same way that there is hierarchy in the natural world, there is hierarchy in the spiritual world. We see that there are thrones, dignities, dominations, authorities and angels, which correspond to the various angelic hierarchical levels. "For in Him [in Jesus] have all things been created **which are in heavens and on earth, the visible** and **the invisible**, thrones, dignities, dominations, authorities" (Colossians 1:16). Later, we will see that all powers in the heavens and on earth have been given to Jesus, the son of God[6]. The angels also are organized in a hierarchy: Seraphim, Cherubim, archangels and angels. Each angel has a specific role, depending on his position. Angels are closest to men, then come archangels. The word archangel comes from the Greek words *archo* and *aggelos*, *archo* meaning "head" and *aggelos* "angel". So, archangels are head angels. Above them are the angels closest to God, cherubim and seraphim, that are close to His throne. Angels are

---

4. Olivier Derain: IBEM course, « Le monde invisible » (Course n°2).
5. Elme-Marie Caro: *L'Idée de Dieu et ses nouveaux critiques,* Ed. Hachette, 1864 (1st edition), 2nd Ed. 2007, p. 396
6. Matthew 28:18.

the spirits who work for God, sent to exercise a ministry for those about to inherit salvation[7]. The mission of angels is to protect, serve and help the children of God in the accomplishment of their mission on earth. They also watch over the people who do not know God yet, but who, when the time comes, will turn to Him. Knowing this, maybe you now realize that at some point in time angels might have rescued you. I experienced this ten years ago, when I was not a Christian yet. I was with some friends and we were heading back home after a night out at the Mondial, a night club in the Netherlands. The party had ended at 5:00 am and we were driving back to Paris without resting. I was driving and after one hour, exhausted, I nodded off and started to dream. In my dream, I could myself driving, with a massive truck driving just ahead of me. As I drove closer to the truck, I panicked and woke up. Simultaneously, the friend on the seat next to mine was calling me. As I opened my eyes, I saw the exact same truck as in my dream... Considering the speed, I could not be alive today telling you this story if I hadn't had that vision.

I didn't realize at the time and thought it was just luck, but today, with hindsight, I am convinced that an angel of God intervened.

- **The Devil**

The Scriptures teach us that one day, Lucifer, a former angel in the service of God, rebelled against His authority. He was a guardian cherub, an Angel close to the throne of God. His name *Lucifer* means "Star light". Contrary to popular imagery in which he is often pictured as having horns

---

7. Hebrews 1:14.

and a fork tail, Lucifer was in fact an extremely beautiful being. It is actually because of his beauty, in addition to the authority and the power given to him by God, that he grew proud and attempted to take God's throne. Ezekiel the prophet tells us how it happened:

> You [the Devil] were anointed as a guardian cherub, for so I ordained you. You were on the holy mount of God; you walked among the fiery stones. You were blameless in your ways from the day you were created till wickedness was found in you. Through your widespread trade you were filled with violence, and you sinned. So I drove you in disgrace from the mount of God, and I expelled you, guardian cherub, from among the fiery stones. Your heart became proud on account of your beauty, and you corrupted your wisdom because of your splendor. So I threw you to the Earth; I made a spectacle of you before kings (Ezekiel 28: 14 to 17)

Because of his pride and his sin, he lost his Cherub status and God ejected him from heaven. His name Lucifer was changed to *Devil*, meaning "slanderer" and to *Satan,* which means "adversary, enemy".

In his fall, he took one-third of the angels[8], established his kingdom in the first and second heavens and formed what we call the kingdom of darkness. His main objective is to destroy God's creation. We will see a bit further that in deceiving Adam and Eve, he managed to reclaim the governance of the Earth. Indeed, in obeying the Devil rather than God, Adam and Eve put themselves under his thumb, as explained in this verse of the Apostle Paul:

> Don't you know that when you offer yourselves to someone as obedient slaves, **you are slaves of the one you obey** - whether you are slaves to sin, which leads to death, or to obedience, which leads to righteousness? (Romans 6:16)

In general, people who do not believe in God neither believe in the Devil, and it is where part of his strength comes from, pretending he does not exist and acting in a hidden manner. However, some actions of Man are so mad and inhumane, that even people who believe in nothing sometimes feel there must be dark forces that influence some individuals to the point of pushing them to commit such atrocities.

---

8. Revelations 12: 4

2 – The role of men and women on earth

> And God said, "Let there be light," and there was light. God saw that the light was good, and he separated the light from the darkness. God called the light "day", and the darkness he called "night." And there was evening, and there was morning - the first day. And God said, "Let there be a vault between the waters to separate water from water." So God made the vault and separated the water under the vault from the water above it. And it was so. God called the vault "sky." And there was evening, and there was morning - the second day. (Genesis 1:3-8)

When one takes time to reflect on the different stages of creation, they notice that nothing has been left to coincidence, but everything was created in sequence and in a specific chronology. Each element of the creation has a well-defined role and obeys a function that is its own. Science is able to explain how some elements of the creation work, but cannot always explain why. However, the Scriptures teach us that the Creator has designed the framework of life, night and day, nature and its elements, and that He has arranged them to be in the service of Man. In the same way that parents prepare a room for the birth of their child, God prepared the Earth to welcome men and women. It is in this continuity that He creates and gives each of them a role within this huge universe, He says to them: "You will be the managers of this Earth":

> Then God said, "Let us make mankind in our image, in our likeness, so that they may **rule over** the fish in the sea and the birds in the sky, over the livestock and all the wild animals, and over all the creatures that move along the ground". (...) "**Be fruitful** and increase in number; **fill** the earth and subdue it. **Rule over** the fish in the sea and the birds in the sky and over every living creature that moves on the ground."
> (Genesis 1:26-28)

After having settled the ideal environment for Adam and Eve, He gave them the responsibility of taking care of it. The order to **subdue the Earth** corresponds to establishing and extending the Kingdom of God on earth.

The Hebrew word for dominate is *radah*, which also means "govern, sovereign reign, subject". Adam and Eve were both responsible for taking care of the environment and manage it. In this passage, the instructions given to them were to multiply, fill the Earth (introduction of the family) and **rule**. Strangely enough, at no point did He tell them how to proceed, considering they were the first beings on earth. We will see later that when God gives responsibility, He gives the capacities that go along with it.

And it is by deploying his capabilities in accordance with the will of God that Man honors his Creator and feels fully accomplished.

- **Man after the fall**

> And the Lord God commanded the man, "You are free to eat from any tree in the garden; but you must not eat from the tree of the knowledge of good and evil, for when you eat from it you will certainly die."
> (Genesis 2:16)

Adam and Eve were in the garden of Eden, in perfect communion with God. The word Eden means "pleasure and delight" in Hebrew. The garden of Eden does not only represent a physical place (which, according to theologians, was located in Mesopotamia, i.e. current Iraq), but a divine atmosphere as well. They were allowed to eat all the fruits of the garden, except those from a specific tree: the tree of the knowledge of good and evil. The Devil seduced and told them: "Has God really told you not to eat of all the trees of the Garden?" (Genesis 3:1). With this simple question, He challenged the Word, the honesty and the holiness of God, by insinuating: "He does not want you to be like Him: gods". Curious and seduced by the arguments the snake (the Devil) was putting forward, they disobeyed and transgressed the divine order in eating some of the fruit, in the hope of being like God. What they were not aware of is that their privileged position with God was already making them *gods* on earth. King David wrote in one of his psalms: "I said, **'You are gods; you are all sons of**

the Most High.'" (Psalm 82:6). This Act of disobedience is equivalent to an act of defiance towards God because in doing so, they showed that they really believed God could lie to them. Their conduct had two fatal consequences on them and all humanity:

- Physical death
- Spiritual death

- **Physical death?**

In Western societies, medical advances have made life extension possible until an average of 78 years for men and 84 years for women. Despite all the methods used to delay aging, it is inevitable: death is an obligatory step for every individual. The attitude of each person in the face of death depends on the person's beliefs.

Atheists deny the existence of God and argue that life ends after death. For them, there is nothing beyond. Many enjoy their time on earth, putting aside all existential questions. This *belief* also leads many of them to enjoy life to the point of burning the candle at both ends. This way of looking at life reminds us of the famous phrase from the Latin poet Horace: "Carpe diem! Enjoy the present day without worrying about the next day". However, at the dawn of life, some questions and doubts keep rising to the surface.

Believers know that there is life after death. Believing opens a perspective on eternity, even though the vision of the hereafter and how to get there may differ from some individuals and religions to others. In the Bible, Jesus is presented as being the only way that leads to heaven:

> **I am the gate**; whoever enters through me will be saved. They will come in and go out, and find pasture. The thief comes only to steal and kill and destroy; **I have come that they may have life, and have it to the full**. I am the good shepherd. The good shepherd lays down his life for the sheep. (John 10:9 to 11)

- **Spiritual death?**

By disobeying God, Adam and Eve broke the link and the special relationship they had with Him. This action destroyed the trust and harmony that prevailed in the Garden, and opened the door to sin, which entered their lives and estranged them away from their Creator. Sin is characterized by disobedience to God and living outside of the plan He has prepared for Man. God has established a good and perfect framework within which peace and joy rule[9]. A framework within which every human being is fully accomplished, by becoming the person they are meant to be, through communion with God. The Hebrew word for sin is *chatta'th*, which means "**to miss the target**", considering the good instructions pre-established by God. Whenever an individual commits a sin, they depart from God's will and perfect plan for their life. And it did not take long to observe the consequences of sin in the heart of men. Just

---

9. Romans 14:17: "For the kingdom of God is not a matter of eating and drinking, but of righteousness, peace and joy in the Holy Spirit."

look at the lives of the two sons of Adam and Eve, Cain and Abel. Cain became jealous because his brother made a better offering than his to the Lord. Jealousy led to murder:

> In the course of time Cain brought some of the fruits of the soil as an offering to the LORD. And Abel also brought an offering - fat portions from some of the firstborn of his flock. The LORD looked with favor on Abel and his offering, but on Cain and his offering he did not look with favor. So, Cain was very angry, and his face was downcast. Then the LORD said to Cain, "Why are you angry? Why is your face downcast? If you do what is right, will you not be accepted? **But if you do not do what is right, sin is crouching at your door; it desires to have you, but you must rule over it**." (Genesis 4:3 to 7)

Rather than pulling himself together, Cain said to Abel: "let's go out to the field" and while they were in the field, **Cain threw himself on his brother Abel** and killed him (Genesis 4:3-8).

By their act of disobedience, Adam and Eve have contaminated all humanity. Their offspring inherited the curse of sin despite themselves. Away from God, Man finds himself subject to his emotions, desires, wants and impulses. Sin kindles anger, hate, aggression, bitterness, animosity, jealousy, resentment, revenge, greed, anxiety anguish, etc.

How many people die every day from the ravages of alcohol, drugs, junk food (second cause of death in the U.S.A.), HIV, reckless drivers, vendetta, rapes, foolish games, fits of anger, murders, diseases due to abuse? How many couples have vowed to love each other for better or worse and have grown to become the worse enemies in the world? Sin acts as power in the human body and pushes one to do or say things they sometimes immediately regret. Unfortunately, this force is stronger than them. This is what the Apostle Paul explains, as he was also confronted with sin in his own life:

> I do not understand what I do. For what I want to do I do not do, but what I hate I do. **And if I do what I do not want to do, I agree that the law is good. As it is, it is no longer I myself who do it, but it is sin living in me.** For I know that good itself does not dwell in me, that is, in my sinful nature. For I have the desire to do what is good, but I cannot carry it out. For I do not do the good I want to do, but the evil I do not want to do - this I keep on doing. Now if I do what I do not want to do, it is no longer I who do it, but it is sin living in me that does it. So I find this law at work: Although I want to do good, evil is right there with me. For in my inner being I delight in God's law; but I see another law at work in me,

waging war against the law of my mind and making me a prisoner of the law of sin at work within me. What a wretched man I am! Who will rescue me from this body that is subject to death? (Romans 7:15-24)

This passage helps us better understand how evil eventually ended up spreading progressively in our hearts, to the point of spreading throughout all societies. It is so entrenched that some behaviors, previously considered as bad, are now acceptable and even good, and other behaviors which were considered as good, are now bad. Yet, God has written the notions of good and bad in every individual's heart, so that their conscience constantly calls them to order, when they commit wrong actions.

Anthropologists who observed societies that have never been in contact with Judeo-Christian thought have found out that they, too, have these notions of good and evil. In the news columns, it is not uncommon to read articles about people who commit a crime and then surrender themselves to the police, overwhelmed by the weight of their own conscience. However, this is becoming less and less common. By constantly repeating the same bad things, the soul eventually adjusts and integrates these actions as being acceptable behaviors. When this happens, the inner voice of conscience becomes a vague inaudible whisper.

3 – The plan of redemption

- **The omniscience of God**

God is omniscient, He knew before creating Adam and Eve that they would disobey Him and lead all humanity to its fall. Yet, He still chose to create them and gave them free will, in other words the ability to decide for themselves what they consider good or bad. His love as a Father is such that His wish is certainly not to create a servile being, but rather sons and daughters who have will and desires.

The plan of redemption for humanity was therefore pre-determined before the formation of the Earth. In creating Man, God also foresaw the way to deliver him from the death of sin and total perdition. That is why, when He found out about Adam and Eve's disobedience, He immediately informed them about the way He would deliver them from sin: He would send **a savior**, born to a woman (so a human being), who would crush the head of the serpent (the Devil), but the latter would injure his heel (wounds of Jesus on the cross). It would be a man from their offspring. Here is what he told them:

> Then the Lord God said to the woman, "What is this you have done?" The woman said, "The serpent deceived me, and I ate." So the Lord God said to the serpent, "Because you have done this, "Cursed are you above all livestock and all wild animals! You will crawl on your belly and you will eat dust all the days of your life. **And I will put enmity between you**

and the woman, and between your offspring and hers; he will crush your head, and you will strike his heel." (Genesis 3:13 to 15)

Away from God, Adam and Eve very quickly realized what they had done and that their living conditions would be totally changed. God later chose a man named Abraham and from his offspring were born many nations. Abraham begat Isaac, who begat Jacob. God changed the name Jacob into Israel. He had twelve sons who formed, with their descendants, the twelve tribes of Israel. Faithful to His covenant with Abraham, He chose these people to reveal Himself to the world by sending the Messiah, the Savior of the world. Thus, throughout the Old Testament, several prophets announced His coming, but none of them knew neither the day nor the hour.

We will now see how God, in His omniscience, had planned to save humanity from the condemnation that was hanging over it and how He would reconcile men to Himself.

- **The absence of God and the condemnation of humanity**

When the time has come for a person to leave the Earth, their body becomes dust and their spirit has two possible destinations: the presence of God or the place where the dead stay, awaiting the final judgement. After the judgement, those who are not judged righteous in the eyes of God are thrown into hell. Hell is a place that was initially reserved for the Devil and his demons. Since, it has become a place of torment for sinners because God, who is Holy, cannot allow them in His presence. The Bible says: "[God] Your eyes are too pure to look on evil; you cannot tolerate wrongdoing." (Habakkuk 1:13).

The Apostle Peter also writes: "But just as he who called you is holy, so be holy in all you do; for it is written: "Be holy, because I am holy." (1 Peter 1:15). Pastor João Martins, who, for many years worked with drug addicts, one day said: "hell is not filled with sinners as many think, but with people who refused to acknowledge God as their adoptive father. Hell is not only characterized by the flames or the heat as we were told to believe for centuries, it is characterized above all else by the absence of the presence of God. If God is Peace, Life and Light, it is therefore consistent that His absence results in torment, death and darkness.

- **God's means of redemption to save humanity**

God decided to release men and women from death and sin through the sacrifice of His son Jesus Christ. The cross is part of the controversial events in History. Much has been written about it. It has caused much blood to be shed and divided many peoples. Very few people deny the fact that Jesus lived on earth, but the points of discord are the fact that He calls Himself the **Son of God** and that the Bible claims that He **rose from the dead**. Jesus came to withdraw the condemnation that rested on humanity. As long as this sentence remained, it was impossible for anyone to be with God for eternity. God, who is Holy and judge of all things, could not break His own law in exculpating men from what they had done. He had to lift the condemnation that weighed on humanity. In other words, he had to deliver His creation that was henceforth doomed to eternal death, because it had sinned in choosing to obey the Devil instead of Him. Let us recall the verse we have seen previously: "Don't you know that when you offer yourselves to someone as obedient slaves, you are slaves of the one you obey (…)." (Romans 6:16).

His creation meant so much to Him and the condemnation of sin weighing on it was so heavy that an "alternative" of inestimable value, someone who would pay the **ransom price** instead of humans in order to release them, had to be found. The ransom was not to be paid to the Devil but to God Himself.

> Just as the Son of Man did not come to be served, but to serve, and **to give his life as a ransom for many**. (Matthew 20:28)

God the Son offered Himself to go to earth. Given the Devil had stolen the governance of the Earth from Adam and Eve, it was necessary that a person of the same nature (a man) would take back what they had lost. So, God the Son was incarnated as a man to perfectly accomplish His mission. By coming to earth, he thus fulfilled the prophecies that heralded His coming. The author of the book of Hebrews relates this exchange between Him and the Father:

> Therefore, when Christ came into the world, he said: "Sacrifice and offering you did not desire, **but a body you prepared for me**; with burnt offerings and sin offerings you were not pleased. Then I said,

'Here I am - it is written about me in the scroll - I have come **to do your will, my God.**'" (Hebrews 10:5-7)

- **Reconciliation with God**

Jesus made the choice, in agreement with his father, to bear the sentence which should have fallen on mankind. This deed is a demonstration of the unconditional love of God the Father and God the Son. God never stopped loving His creation, and continues to look upon it as a father over his children. The Bible says: "For God so loved the world that he gave **his one and only Son**, that whoever believes in him shall not perish but have eternal life." (John 3:16). In coming to earth, God the Son left His skies of glory and lowered Himself to the level of men[10] and took upon Himself the form of man. The Bible says: "For in Christ all the fullness of the Deity lives in bodily form," (Colossians 2:9). Despite the refusal of Jesus' opponents to believe that He was the Son of God, they nevertheless acknowledged, through the extraordinary works He did - miracles, healings, the resurrection of the dead - that the hand of God was with Him. It was inconceivable to them that the Son of God would come among them as a simple man, with no pageantry, no wealth and no glory. By killing Him, they were not aware that they were fulfilling the Father's plan: to offer His beloved Son as a sacrifice to save humanity. Isaiah the prophet, 700 years before the coming of the Messiah, wrote the following: "But he was pierced for our

---

10. He Himself speaks about the glory He once had near the Father: "And now, Father, glorify me in your presence with the glory I had with you before the world began."

transgressions, he was crushed for our iniquities; the punishment that brought us peace was on him, and by his wounds we are healed." (Isaiah 53:5)

John the Baptist, when seeing Him, had declared: "Look, the Lamb of God, who takes away the sin of the world!" (John 1:29). His death did not go unnoticed. During His crucifixion, there was darkness over the entire surface of the Earth from noon until 3:00 pm and when He died, people there could only realize that was indeed the Son of God. Matthew, one of His disciples, related this event:

> At that moment the curtain of the temple was torn in two from top to bottom. The Earth shook, the rocks split and the tombs broke open. The bodies of many holy people who had died were raised to life. They came out of the tombs after Jesus' resurrection and went into the holy city and appeared to many people. **When the centurion and those with him who were guarding Jesus saw the earthquake and all that had happened, they were terrified, and exclaimed, "Surely he was the Son of God!"** (Matthew 27:51 to 54)

But three days after His death, an uncommon event shook the entire region. Jesus rose from the dead, as announced by the Scriptures. He appeared to Mary of Magdala, to the disciples and to more than 500 persons at once[11]. Others also witnessed His resurrection. Having not sinned while on earth, the place of the dead (Sheol) could not keep Him, because it was a place for sinners only. Through the cross, God had overturned the conviction that was weighing on the creation. The Apostle Paul says: "When you were dead in your sins and in the uncircumcision of your flesh, God made you alive with Christ. He forgave us all our sins, having canceled the charge of our legal indebtedness, which stood against us and condemned us; he has taken it away, nailing it to the cross." (Colossians 2:13 and 14). He also states:

> **And through him to reconcile to himself** all things, whether things on earth or things in heaven, **by making peace through his blood**, shed on the cross. Once you were alienated from God and were enemies in your minds because of your evil behavior. But now he has reconciled you by Christ's physical body through death to **present you holy in his sight, without blemish and free from accusation** (Colossians 1:20-22)

The blood of Jesus needed to flow, because He alone has the power to redeem men from death and sin. The Apostle John says, on this subject: "The blood of Jesus, his Son, purifies us from all sin." (1 John 1:7), and he adds "he

---

11. 1 Corinthians 15:6.

[Jesus] is the atoning sacrifice for our sins, and not only for ours but also for the sins of the whole world." (1 John 2:2). Jesus gave His life for the Salvation of the world and declared Himself to be the only way to the Father. He said: «I am the way, the truth and the life. No one comes to the Father but by me". (John 14:6). Many works of excellent quality have been written in this regard[12], therefore I do not intend to go into detail, but simply explain that God the Father always had this desire to save His creation. Mankind finds it hard to apprehend that God the Son would make Himself man, consequently of the same nature as us and that He gave His life to **save** humanity, because this is completely irrational to the human intellect. To understand this reality, one needs to receive a revelation from the Holy Spirit. Even today, salvation is offered to all, free of charge, without any merit. This may seem incomprehensible to some, in a society where we are used to receiving upon merit. Salvation is not based on the works we can accomplish, our social status, the color of our skin, our culture, but it is simply given by grace. Salvation is offered to all: it is God's grace. Grace is a favor a person receives, while having done nothing to deserve it. The Bible says: "It's by the grace indeed that you are saved, through faith. And is not from yourselves, it is a gift of God. It is not of works so that no one can boast." (Ephesians 2:8-9)

---

12. The book *Jesus, Prendre plaisir à le découvrir* (La Maison de la Bible, 2007) by John Piper is a wonderful example of this fact.

Chapter 2
A new spiritual beginning

1 – The new birth

New birth occurs in one's life when they realize they are nothing without God and acknowledge with all their heart that they need Him to be released from their condition and saved. It thus happens when they believe that Jesus is the Son of God, that He died on the cross for their sins and that He is the only one able to save them. New birth is effective to anyone who confesses with their mouth that they accept Jesus Christ as Lord and Savior, and give Christ access to their life. The Apostle Paul said: "If you confess with your mouth the Lord Jesus, and if you believe in your heart that God has risen Him from the dead, you will be saved" (Romans 10:9). This simple prayer, said with a sincere heart invites the Spirit of God to take up residence in the heart of the person who made the statement. The presence of the Holy Spirit in their life brings their spirit back to life and awakens them to spiritual realities. Here is what the Scriptures say about this: "I will give you a new heart and put a new spirit in you. I will remove from your body the heart of stone and give you a heart of flesh." (Ezekiel 36:26). This person's mind then becomes alive and is awakened to spiritual things, when receiving the Holy Spirit. This increased awareness leads to repentance. The Greek word used in the Bible for repentance is *metanoia*. *Metanoia* means "change of mentality, of intent". Repentance happens when a sincere heart acknowledges being on the wrong track.

Awareness leads us to take a new direction, but not just any: the one that leads to life, peace and joy of the soul.

- **The true believers**

The expression "to be a believer" has been overused. Many "believe" with their intellect but have strictly no communion with God. Believing is not enough to be called a child of God and be saved. The Apostle James said: "If you believe there is only one God, you do well; demons believe the same and they tremble" (James 2:19). God does not look at denominations (Catholic, Protestant, Evangelical, Adventist, Baptist, etc.). He sees as His children those in whom the Holy Spirit resides. The only guarantee for the believer to inherit eternal life is to make sure the Spirit of God dwells in their heart.

> And you also were included in Christ when you heard the message of truth, the gospel of your salvation. When you believed, you were marked in him with a seal, the promised Holy Spirit, **who is a deposit guaranteeing our inheritance** until the redemption of those

> who are God's possession - to the praise of his glory. (Ephesians 1:13-14)

How sure are you? The Holy Spirit certifies the believer's spirit that he or she is a child of God:

> For those who are led by the Spirit of God are the **children of God**. The Spirit you received does not make you slaves, so that you live in fear again; rather, the Spirit you received brought about your adoption to sonship. And by him we cry, *"Abba,* Father." **The Spirit himself testifies with our spirit that we are God's children.**(Romans 8:14-16)

2 – A new identity in Christ

- **Change of identity**

When the Spirit of God comes to dwell in the heart of a person, they become what is called a **child of God**. That person inherits the identity God had granted them when He created them and, discovering this new identity as well as the plans and projects God has in store for them will be the most exciting adventure of their entire life. We will deal with this in the fourth part of this book, entitled "Destiny".

Salvation becomes their inheritance; the fear of death vanishes and a new life begins. A life of peace, not of misfortune, with a future and hope[1].

- **Enjoy reading the Bible**

The presence of the Holy Spirit in one's life triggers joy from reading the Bible and hearing the Word of God. The Bible which previously appeared to many as just a story book, little by little becomes a book of revelations within which one gradually understands the mysteries of God. The Holy Scriptures become alive, they answer their many questions, reassure them, strengthen their faith, help them move forward in life, reveal God's heart and connect them to the source of Life: Jesus Christ.

- **The hidden mysteries in the Word of God**

"The glory of God, is to hide things; the glory Kings, is to probe things." (Proverbs 25:2)

God has hidden His mysteries from men, but reveals them to His children. Without the Holy Spirit, the understanding of God's Word is purely intellectual. It neither produces change nor transformation. I have had the opportunity to discuss with people who were very knowledgeable about the Bible. They could quote verses and stand their ground in a debate. But their understanding was merely intellectual: they had received no revelation of God's Word. Who, better than the author Himself, can tell you about the book

---

1. Jeremiah 29:11

He has written? "All Scripture is inspired of God"[2], given to the heart of the apostles and prophets by the Holy Spirit, who in turn have simply transcribed the mind of God.

3 – A life transformed

- **Letting go of the bad habits you were captive of**

  New birth induces change. Some even call it an upheaval, in the way of seeing and perceiving life. Habits they were attached to now seem futile and meaningless. Other things they once did, said or partook now make them feel uncomfortable, because their conscience has been called to order. An inner struggle begins between their new identity, that is coming into existence and the former, that has been expelled but attempts to still be in control. In order to permanently shut the door to a former identity, one must imperatively change their way of thinking and acting. They need to stop looking back and must position themselves into a life of sanctification. For some, the change radically occurs, while for others it is progressive, this varying upon the person's character and the level of acceptance regarding their new life.

Let us imagine a person used to committing fraud in public transport, lying to customers to ensure sales, poorly talking about friends and family behind their backs, etc., without any rebuke from anyone. When the change occurs, the same person will suddenly feel embarrassed and uncomfortable every time the bad action is performed. When this happens, it is a good thing. It is the evident result of the

---

2. 2 Timothy 3:16

transforming power of the Holy Spirit in the person's life. Some habits or addictions are more persistent, because they triumph over the individual's will.

Whenever the temptation comes, their pulse accelerates, the urge increases and it is as if they were driven by an inner force. The person would often say: "I can't resist it, it's stronger than me!". The Apostle Peter teaches us: "Every one of us is a slave to that which has triumphed over us"[3]. When it comes to addictions, they often have effects on the body and the flesh, the body being accustomed to the effects and pleasures procured by the addiction. It pushes the individual to do it again and again. When the person is aware of the situation, it is already a small victory, for many believe they are in control of their will, while when we look at them it is obvious that they are tied to their addictions. There are many examples: addiction to medication, drugs, alcohol, pornography, sex, food, etc.

- **Overcome sin with the help of the Holy Spirit**

"For I do not do the good I want to do, but the evil I do not want to do - this I keep on doing. Now if I do what I do not want to do, it is no longer I who do it, but it is sin living in me that does it." (Romans 7:19-20)

In these verses, the Apostle Paul shows us how hard it is for humans to combat sin, because it is rooted in the human body: "I do not do the good I want, and I do the wrong I do not want to". The human body is contaminated, the carnal man is dominated by his flesh, it controls his will and pushes him to do things that are stronger than him.

---

3. 2 Peter 2:19

The battle of the born-again man or woman takes place at the level of their soul. There is a permanent battle between the spirit and the flesh. The stronger the spirit, the more it dominates the soul and consequently controls the body. To overcome sin, one has to learn to live not according to the flesh, but according to the Spirit. This is what the Apostle Paul teaches the Galatians:

> So, I say, walk by the Spirit, and you will not gratify the desires of the flesh. For the flesh desires what is contrary to the Spirit, and the Spirit what is contrary to the flesh. They are in conflict with each other, so that you are not to do whatever you want. (Galatians 5:16-17)

- **What should I do?**

One of the first things is to desire to be free, whether it is because of an addiction, personality issues or past wounds... The second thing is to admit that you cannot make it alone and that you need the help of the Holy Spirit. The third is to break the habits that have taken roots in your intelligence, in your soul. The Apostle Paul, who knew the human nature well, wrote a letter to the Romans in which he explained the importance of renewing their mind. He told them:" Do not be conformed to the things of this world, **but be transformed by the renewing of your mind** so that you may discern what the will of God is, that which is good, pleasing and perfect" (Romans 12:2). In the original version, the Greek word used for transformation is *metamorphoo*, which means "change in another form, transform, transfigured, transformed". This is exactly the same word that is used to describe the process, the metamorphosis of a butterfly. Science also calls it the transformation of the caterpillar into a butterfly: a complete metamorphosis. This mutation from the caterpillar to the butterfly is a perfect illustration of the sinner called to be transformed into the image of Christ. The transformation of the old thinking pattern makes every man and every woman someone new, in harmony with their new identity. Change is possible only through the workings of the Holy Spirit in every believer's life, because men cannot change by their own powers. Let us find out together who the Holy Spirit and His ministry on earth are.

Chapter 3
Between the Holy Spirit and Man

1 – The Trinity

God reveals Himself through three separate entities, it is the Trinity. While we are spirit, soul and body, God reveals Himself through three equal persons: God the Father, God the Son and God the Holy Spirit.

Nicolas Bergier's Dictionary of Theology defines the "Trinity" as follows: "The unit of three divine persons with regard to nature, and their real distinction with regard to personality"[1]. This notion of Trinity is a mystery which to this day is not easy to apprehend, because it is not evident for one to understand that there is only one God, revealed in three persons. While all three are identical and of the same nature, they do not have the same functions.

---

1. Nicolas Bergier: *Dictionary of Theology*, 1844, p. 22.

- **Presentation of the Trinity:**

The Bible does not directly use the word" Trinity" to define these three entities, but expresses it through several verses, including from the first lines of the book of Genesis: "In the beginning, **God** created the heavens and the Earth" (Genesis 1:1). In this passage, the Hebrew word for God is *Elohim*, which means "gods" (in the plural form). Only the original Hebrew text highlights that the first verse of the Scriptures was not speaking of God the Father only, but referring to the Trinity. The same use of the name Elohim appears in the following passage:" Then **God** said: Let us make man in our image, to our likeness." (Genesis 1:26).

On several occasions in the Bible, God also uses the first person plural pronoun **"us"** to speak of **"Him"**. He does it when He creates man: "Then **God** said: '**Let Us make** man in **our** image, to our likeness!'" (Genesis 1:26). Let us now look at how these three persons are distinctly defined.

The **Father** exists from eternity. When He comes to Moses, He says: "I am that I am" (Exodus 3:14). That is to say, "I am the Lord". The corresponding Hebrew word is *Yehovah* or *Yaweh*.

The **Son** is the Word, the Word of God: "In the beginning was the Word, and the Word was with God, and the Word was God." (John 1:1). He is the Creator of the heavens and the Earth: "In Him [the Son] were all things created that are in the heavens and on the Earth, the visible and the invisible (…). Everything was created by Him and for Him." (Colossians 1:16). And as we have seen previously, the Son became incarnate in Jesus Christ: "And the Word has been made flesh, and dwelt among us, full of grace and truth, and we beheld His glory, as the glory of the only Son sent from the Father." (John 1:14).

The Holy Spirit is the comforter promised by Jesus, the Spirit of God who accompanies the children of God every day.

Thus, each person within the Trinity has a well-defined role. Let us take a simple example to understand the role of each. Let us imagine the construction of a house, within which each member of the Trinity intervenes:

- **God the Father** represents the authority, the One who has the vision. To use a more explicit term, we could see him as the "Director".

- **God the Son** creates, schedules, formats and transforms the thought of the Father into reality. He could be compared to the "Architect".

- **God the Holy Spirit** brings into existence what Jesus asks Him. He could be called the "Foreman".

- **God takes three forms**

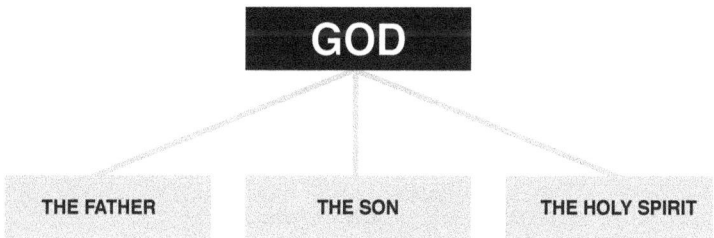

To complete your understanding, we can also use the image of water. **Water comes in three forms**. It can be at once liquid, solid and vapor. No matter the form, it is still water.

If the representation of God the Father and God the Son is easy, it is intellectually more complex when it comes to understanding the person of the Holy Spirit. Let us look at it together.

2 – The person of the Holy Spirit

The Holy Spirit is neither strength nor power. It is a person and it is the least known person of the Trinity, even among believers. Yet, when looking at the Scriptures carefully, we note that it is the first person of the Trinity to clearly be identified, from the second verse of the book of Genesis:

> Now the Earth was formless and empty, darkness was over the surface of the deep, and **the Spirit of God was hovering over the waters**. (Genesis 1:2)

As He was going up to heaven, Jesus promised His disciples that He would send them *another comforter*, that would always be with them, until eternity. He said:

> I have much more to say to you, more than you can now bear. But when he, the Spirit of truth, comes, he will guide you into all the truth. He will not speak on his own; he will speak only what he hears, and he will tell you what is yet to come. He will glorify me because it

is from me that he will receive what he will make known to you. (John 16:12-14)

The Greek word for comforter is *parakletos*, which means "an assistant, a lawyer, an advisor". Due to lack of knowledge, there is a tendency to believe that the Holy Spirit is a power or force. However, the Holy Spirit is a divine person. A person with emotions and feelings. Several verses in the Holy Scriptures underline His sensitivity: "Grieve not the Holy Spirit" (Ephesians 4:10). The Holy Spirit counsels, teaches, consoles, communicates peace, joy and divine wisdom. In sending His Spirit, God took up residence in the heart of His children, in order to constantly be with them. The Apostle Paul tells us: "Do you not know that you are the temple of the Holy Spirit and that the Spirit of God dwells in you?" (1 Corinthians 3:16). The presence of the Holy Spirit in a believer's heart allows them to have God within themselves to accomplish His plans and implement His teachings. It is important to always keep in mind that even Jesus, when He was on earth, accomplished signs, healings and miracles, thanks to the Holy Spirit and His close collaboration with the Father. He Himself says:

> "Very truly I tell you**, the Son can do nothing by himself; he can do only what he sees his Father doing,** because whatever the Father does the Son also does. (John 5:19)

> You know how **God anointed Jesus of Nazareth with the Holy Spirit and power**, and how he went

around doing good and healing all who were under the power of the Devil, because God was with him. (Acts 10:38)

Each person of the Trinity willingly works in perfect harmony. The revelation of the sons and daughters of God is possible only through the **knowledge** and the **communion** they develop day after day with the person of the Holy Spirit. It is through this relationship that the man and woman of God are transformed into the image of Christ and quickly manifest His character and His works, in different occasions of their life.

The Holy Spirit is given to believers to establish a direct relationship with God, which emphasizes the importance of communion, because there cannot be friendship without exchange. The Apostle Paul completed his second epistle to the Corinthians by saying:" May the grace of the Lord Jesus Christ, the love of God, the **communion** of the Holy Spirit be with you." (2 Corinthians 13:13). He insisted on the need to be "connected" to the Holy Spirit. Each of us meets different people throughout the day, and our exchanges vary, depending on how close we are to those we meet. We can say that there are three levels of intimacy:

- **Level 1: the relationship**

    It is characterized by easy and safe conversations, **exchange of information** without feelings, opinions or personal vulnerability. This is the type of interaction one can have with a stranger.

- **Level 2: communion**

    It is impossible to be in communion with someone without having at least one thing in common. A person is in communion with God when they have something in common with Him. To this end, one should stop focusing on their own self, needs and personal interests but rather look towards God instead and allow Him to be part of their life.

    When two companies merge, they cannot keep their initial state. They change names and legal status. The same applies to the communion with God. Consecration, faith, holiness are all common points that **make a communion with God possible.**

- **Level 3: intimacy**

    When two persons are united, they become intimate and there is no more secrets between them. Communion brings intimacy and intimacy strengthens communion. God reveals His secrets to those who are close to Him. This is also what this passage from the Scriptures reminds us: "**The friendship of the Lord is for those who fear him, and he makes known to them his covenant.**" (Psalms 25: 14). The use of "to fear" in this verse does not mean "to be afraid", or "to be terrorized" by God, but "to have respect, reverence".

3 – The baptism of the Holy Spirit

Just before being taken to heaven, Jesus recommended His disciples not to leave Jerusalem, but stay there until they would receive what had been promised by the Father: The baptism of the Holy Spirit.

Indeed, to perfectly fulfill the mission that had been entrusted to them, the disciples needed to first receive the baptism of the Holy Spirit. A few days later, while they were gathering in an upper room, the Holy Spirit fell on them and they all began to speak new languages.

The peculiarity of speaking in tongues is that: "For anyone who speaks in a tongue does not speak to people but to God. Indeed, no one understands them; they utter mysteries by the Spirit." (1Corinthians 14:2). We will see in further detail the meaning of speaking in tongues when we deal with the gifts of the Spirit. Like in the case of the Apostle Peter, the baptism of the Holy Spirit brings an immediate and radical transformation. The one who previously denied Jesus three times, out of fear of the authorities, was now standing in front of a crowd, speaking with boldness and confidence. The power of the Holy Spirit had freed him from all his fears. It also helped him overcome the departure of his leader. As we saw previously, every person who is born again receives the Holy Spirit **in them**. On the other hand, the one who is baptized in the Holy Spirit witnesses it coming **on them**. It is important to make this distinction, because the presence of the Holy Spirit inside the heart of the believer is for **their salvation**, while the Holy Spirit onto them is **for the salvation of those who surround them**.

The baptism of the Holy Spirit is not an end in itself. Any believer who receives it must keep developing their communion with God, in order to discover and use the gifts received and thus manifest the power of God. This communion progressively brings a change in one's way of thinking and reasoning, and allows them to "synchronize" their thoughts with the thoughts of God, their spirit with the Spirit of God, their perspective with that of God. The spirit of the believer somehow becomes the gateway between earth and the heavens, between the natural and the supernatural. The more the believer strengthens their mind, the greater their faith and the more they become aware of the realities of the kingdom of God. Pastor Bill Johnson of Bethel Church in California talks about the importance of developing one's mind in one of his books:

> The spirit is the essential tool to bring the reality of the Kingdom in the problems and the crises faced by people. God designed it to be the gateway to the supernatural. But to be useful in the Kingdom, our thoughts must be transformed (...) When they are transformed, not only our thoughts are different, but so is our way of thinking, because **we** think from a different reality: **from the heavens** to the **Earth**.[2]

---

2. Bill Johnson: *The Supernatural power of a transformed mind*, Ed. Destiny, p. 42.

4 – Be filled with the Holy Spirit

Nowadays, there are more and more believers in the world, but their lives do not always impact our societies as they should. When reading the Acts of the Apostles and discovering the beginnings of the Church, we see that the disciples witnessed miracles, extraordinary healings and crowd conversion. The impact was such that Christianity spread throughout the Roman Empire.

Some people think this time is now behind us. Others, however, believe that the promises made by Jesus are real: "Very truly I tell you, whoever believes in me will do the works I have been doing, and they will do even greater things than these, because I am going to the Father." (John 14:12) but cannot experience them. When looking at the first disciples and apostles, we see that a particular element characterized them: **they were filled with the Holy Spirit.** Let us look together at two examples:

> After they prayed, the place where they were meeting was shaken. **And they were all filled with the Holy Spirit** and spoke the word of God boldly. (Acts 4:31)

> "They chose Stephen, a man **full of faith and of the Holy Spirit.**" (Acts 6:5). And a little further down in verse 8: "Now Stephen, a man **full of God's grace and power,** performed great wonders and signs among the people."

No believer can fully accomplish the will of God unless they are filled with the Holy Spirit. They limp, using their own strength, and their life is not as meaningful as the one calling them. That is why the Church does not exert its influence as it should. Paul invited the believers of the city of Ephesus to be filled with the Holy Spirit. He told them: "Do not get drunk on wine, which leads to debauchery. **Instead, be filled with the Spirit.**" (Ephesians 5:18).

The Greek word used in this verse for filled is *plêroô*, which means "full to the brim" – to be filled with the presence of the Holy Spirit. The theologian John MacArthur uses the following example to explain what "to be filled with the Holy Spirit" means. He says:

> The Christian who is filled with the Spirit can be compared to a glove. When there is no hand in it, a glove has no strength and is useless. It was made to work, but it cannot do it on its own. It does something only insofar as the hand that is in it, controls it and acts. The only work that is done by the glove is the work of the hand. (…) A Christian that is not filled with the Holy Spirit cannot accomplish anything, just like a glove without a hand in it can do nothing.[3]

---

3. John MacArthur: *Ephésiens, Les commentaires bibliques,* Ed. Impact, p. 326.

- **How can one be filled with the Holy Spirit?**

    - By walking in sanctification.

    - By walking in obedience: submitting to the perfect will of God.

    - By reading the Word of God and abiding by it: **be filled with the Word to a point where it transforms the character, the attitude, the thoughts and the prospects for the believer.**

    - By "speaking to one another with psalms, hymns and songs." (Ephesians 5:19)

    - By always being conscious of the presence of God by one's side, and by living each day with that in mind.

So that the people of God deeply transform our society and make God visible within themselves, there is no secret: each child of God must be filled with the Holy Spirit. It is then, and only then, that God will become a reality to our fellow citizens.

5 – The fruit of the Spirit

"But the **fruit of the Spirit** is love, joy, peace, forbearance, kindness, goodness, faithfulness, gentleness and self-control." (Galatians 5:22)

The revelation of the sons and daughters of God implies the manifestation of the **fruit of the Spirit**, as well as that of the **gifts of the Spirit** they have received. The fruit of the Spirit fully testifies of the *presence and character of*

Christ in the life of the believer, and **the gifts demonstrate the power of God.** The more the believer grows in faith, the more the transformation of their character and attitude will become visible, through the love, joy, peace and goodness they demonstrate. The Apostle Paul says: "And hope does not put us to shame, **because God's love has been poured out into our hearts through the Holy Spirit, who has been given to us.**" (Romans 5:5). Love is the very essence of the nature of God. This is what is recorded in 1 Corinthians chapter 13 and verse 4:

> Love is patient, love is kind. It does not envy, it does not boast, it is not proud. It does not dishonor others, it is not self-seeking, it is not easily angered, it keeps no record of wrongs. Love does not delight in evil but rejoices with the truth. It always protects, always trusts, always hopes, always perseveres.

If all the characteristics of the fruit of the Spirit were manifested in the lives of citizens, we would certainly see the country's general atmosphere change very shortly.

6 – The spiritual gifts

> Now to each one the manifestation of the Spirit is given for the common good. To one there is given through the Spirit a **message of wisdom**, to

another a **message of knowledge** by means of the same Spirit, to another **faith** by the same Spirit, to another the **gift of healing** by that one Spirit, to another **miraculous powers**, to another **prophecy**, to another **distinguishing between spirits**, to another speaking in different kinds of tongues, and to still another the **interpretation of tongues**. (1 Corinthians 12:7-10)

These gifts are granted by the Holy Spirit, in a supernatural and sovereign way, to every believer born again. It is not a matter of seeking them but rather receiving them. There are nine gifts. Each child of God receives one or more when they are baptized in the Holy Spirit. They foster mutual edification and manifest the glory of God within our families, friends and entourage. The gifts of the Spirit are divided into three groups of three[4]:

1. **The gifts of inspiration:** prophecy, diversity of tongues, interpretation of tongues.

2. **The gifts of power:** faith, miracle and healing.

3. **The gifts of revelation:** the word of wisdom, word of knowledge, discernment of spirits.

  ▶ **The gift of prophecy** is a gift of inspiration by which the Holy Spirit communicates the Word of God through an individual,

---

4. This point is inspired by the course entitled "Bible classes: the nine gifts of the spirit", given by Pastor Claude Payan.

in order to build, encourage and exhort. Every child of God is called to prophesy, but not everyone is a prophet. The Prophet is a spokesperson, a messenger established and authorized by God to communicate His will and His thought to men.

A couple of years ago, a CEO friend was constantly faced with cash related problems because of the social charges and start-up costs of her new activity. One day, while we were several, praying altogether, a prophet friend told her: "Before the year ends, you will miraculously receive a sum of 20,000 euros for your company". A few days before the year ended, his associate, who knew about the financial problems, injected 20,000 euros into the company's accounts, while he had no knowledge of the prophecy. We can therefore say that she received this money in a miraculous way, because the business partner had actually just recovered it, after lending it a few years prior.

▶ **The gift of diversity of tongues** can be manifested in three ways:

- **Speaking in tongues**: the believer receives this gift when they are baptized in the Holy Spirit. We saw earlier that "anyone who speaks in a tongue does not speak to people but to God. Indeed, no one understands them; they utter mysteries by the Spirit". (1 Corinthians 14:2). Speaking in tongues benefits the one who practices it regularly. If we were to remember three points, I would say that:

- Speaking in tongues allows the one who received the gift to speak directly to the Father's heart, since they don't understand what they themselves say.
- Speaking in tongues helps edify one's spirit: "those who speak in tongues edify themselves." (1 Corinthians 14:3)
- Speaking in tongues helps develop one's communion with God, by having a better understanding of the Word and a greater revelation of the mysteries of God.

One of the keys of the Apostle Paul's powerful ministry and rich revelations was the fact that he spent a lot of time speaking in tongues. He says himself: "I thank God that I speak in tongues more than you all." (1 Corinthians 14:18).

I would recommend those who want to better understand this point to read the excellent book written by Glenn Arekion on this subject, entitled "The Power of Speaking in Tongues"[5].

- **The gift of speaking other spiritual languages or even foreign languages:** This gift gives the ability to speak other spiritual languages, but also master a foreign language, without having ever studied it.

---

5. Glenn Arekion: *La Puissance du Parler en Langues, Ed.* Vida, p.166.

During a Sunday worship service that I was attending, the pastor told us that one day, a believer gave a spiritual gift to the Assembly, during the period of prayer. At the end of the gathering, a new man, of African origin, went to see that person, because the message that he had delivered was in a language that was exactly matching the dialect of his village. He had understood the significance of the message and clearly knew that this message was addressed to him.

- **The interpretation of tongues**: this consists of publicly giving the meaning of a spiritual gift that has been given in tongues, during a gathering. This type of spiritual gift is driven by the Spirit, in order to build up the Church and convince the non-believers, speaking directly to them. If we take the above example, this is equivalent to translating a spiritual gift that has been given in tongues into an intelligible language. Only the Holy Spirit can give the interpretation.

▶ **The gift of faith** is given at a specific time for an exceptional situation that requires a measure of extraordinary faith. When this occurs, the Holy Spirit convinces people that what is impossible according to men is possible for God.

Several testimonies talk about people who were dead, the people at their side being convinced that they would resurrect. They then received a measure of extraordinary faith, prayed, and the deceased resurrected.

▶ **The gift of miracles** is beyond natural belief. It consists of carrying out something that is naturally impossible and unimaginable. Several times, the Bible relates miraculous facts such as the multiplication of the loaves and fish (John 6:7-12) for thousands of people, the separation of the Jordan waters (Joshua 3:14-17) and the Red Sea (Exodus 14:21-29).

▶ **The gift of healing** will, as suggests, cure diseases, disabilities, malformations, etc. Although it is true that each believer is called to pray for the sick and believes they can be healed, the one that has a gift of healing wears a special anointing when praying for the sick.

For example, one day, a group of brothers and sisters went to visit a couple whose wife, approximately in her 50's, was suffering from a very severe kyphosis (she was hunchbacked). Her legs and arms were crippled, cysts in the knees and huge difficulties to move and lift her arms. After having discussed with them and spoken about Jesus, they offered the woman to pray for her. A sister named Felicity laid hands on her and as she was praying, a strong presence of the Holy Spirit was felt in the room. They all witnessed a miracle. They first heard the cracking of the bones and saw the right leg straighten, then her left leg. The swellings on her knees disappeared right away. The hump on her back miraculously melted, she stood straight and began to walk, with no difficulty. She lifted her arms to the heavens but with difficulty, because they were twisted. They prayed for her arms and as for her legs, the bones and muscles straightened and both her arms were straight. The husband was stunned, tears in his eyes: his wife was totally healed. The power of God had just been manifested.

> ▶ **The word of wisdom** is the gift that God uses to communicate a portion of his wisdom to someone, in order to give a revelation, a solution or a clarification on a very specific situation or regarding plans and projects the person expects to perform in the future. The person who gets a word of wisdom recognizes that this word comes from God, due to the depth and accuracy of the revelation. This revelation allows one to have supernatural breakthroughs in areas where it was previously very complicated.

While I was attending a conference, a man of God said that one of his friends was at a business meeting with senior officials of his company. They were looking for a solution to a problem. He was listening without a word, then shared a solution he had just received. When he started to speak, silence filled the room because he was bringing the perfect solution to their problem. His colleagues had no idea, but he had just shared a word from the Holy Spirit, a word of wisdom.

> ▶ **The word of knowledge** is a supernatural revelation of situations, events, past or present things, in someone's life. The Holy Spirit brings these hidden things to light not to condemn the person but rather bring deliverance, healing and revelation of themselves. The word of knowledge brings

revelation about past or present things, while the word of wisdom brings revelation about coming things.

One Sunday morning in church during prayer time, one of my friends, named Kanda, started to feel electric power along his spine. As it was getting stronger and stronger, he understood that the Holy Spirit was telling him that someone was suffering from back pains. He spoke up and said: "Someone is having problems in the spine area. Today is your day to be healed. Receive this healing by faith!" He was told later, at the end of worship, that a person told the pastor it was her and that she was instantly healed.

> ▶ **The discernment of spirits** is a revelation gift through which the Holy Spirit gives the believer the ability to perceive the spiritual world and the world of spirits (angels and demons), as well as the true nature of things according to the eye of God. It is about seeing the invisible of God, it is a spiritual equipment that allows one to discern what is of flesh and what is of spirit. A person who has the gift of discernment of spirits can identify the author of a supernatural event or knows the nature of the spirit that inspires, motivates, agitates, or torments a person.

One of my friends was suffering from a generational curse. At the time of her deliverance, a person who had the gift of discernment could perceive the hiding unclean spirit through the eyes of the Holy Spirit. He therefore spoke directly to that spirit, calling it by its name and ordered it to leave, while proclaiming the name of Jesus. The unclean spirit, knowing that it had been exposed, left within a few minutes.

THIRD PART

Begin living a victorious life

Chapter 1
Be released from the past

This era is marked by a multitude of antagonisms. A large number of people do not believe in the Devil and yet the interest for the occult and demonic things continues to grow, to name but one example. Indeed, in searching for a meaning to their life, several have gotten lost in the occult, the esoteric, and other forms of mystical spirituality.

Because of these practices, a lot of people have spiritual links, even curses they have inherited from their ancestors (family curses, maledictions, etc.) or as a result of their own conscious or unconscious actions. At this point in the book, I think it is necessary to address this issue in order to inform those who, unknowingly, could have exposed themselves to a curse. It is essential to be completely free of past errors, to fully blossom as a son or daughter of God.

1 – The weight of curses

According to the online encyclopaedia Wikipedia, a curse is a "state of inevitable doom which seems to be imposed by a deity, a spell or fate". It is a cycle of bad luck that inevitably repeats itself in the life of a person, a family, or even a nation. Teacher Derek Prince wrote a book entitled "Blessings or curses", in which he gives the following definition:

> A curse could be compared to a long evil arm stretched from our past. It rests on you with a dark and oppressing force which inhibits the full expression of your personality. You never feel completely free to be yourself[1].

Some families have problems with alcoholism from generation to generation, others suffer from the same diseases, others keep failing in everything they do, etc. This grip weighs on these families for several generations, and none seems to know how to release themselves from it. When one member of the family seems to escape from it, it catches up with them after a while. Some nations seem to be building up social misfortune and natural disasters. When these negative things happen again and again, one needs to ask the right questions in order to discern whether beyond the repetitive character, it could not be a curse. The Bible being the prime book that teaches on the laws and principles of God, let us look at an example: the people of Israel, at the time of King David, to illustrate this point:

> During the reign of David, there was a famine for three successive years; so David sought the face of the LORD. The LORD said, "It is on account

---

1. See *Blessing or Curse*, from Derek Prince, p. 13.

> of Saul and his blood-stained house; it is because he put the Gibeonites to death. (2 Samuel 21:1)

It had been three years since the people of Israel were hit by famine. Not knowing what to do, King David consulted God who revealed to him that King Saul, his predecessor, had not respected the alliance concluded 400 years earlier with Joshua, the successor of Moses, and the people of the Gibeonites. Joshua had sworn on oath in the Name of the Lord that he would not attack the Gibeonites (Joshua 9:19), but King Saul had violated that agreement by destroying them. By his deeds, not only did he desecrate the Name of God but he also cursed the entire nation. David, who had nothing to do with that as the new King had to fix his predecessor's mistake to remove the curse and end the famine.

2 – Where do curses come from?

Several sources can attract curses that will lay upon people, families or nations. Let us look at them one by one.

- **Disobedience to the prescriptions given by God**

In the book of Deuteronomy, chapter 28, God speaks to Moses and gives him a list of prescriptions that the Jewish people must follow if he wants to be blessed:

> If you fully obey the Lord your God and carefully follow all his commands I give you today, the Lord your God

will set you high above all the nations on earth. **All these blessings** will come on you and accompany you if you obey the Lord your God: (...). (Deuteronomy 28: 1)

The first fourteen verses list a series of blessings. On the other hand, from verse 15, God lists the misfortunes that will hit those who do not obey His prescriptions. Here is what He said to Moses:

However, if you do not obey the Lord your God and do not carefully follow all his commands and decrees I am giving you today, **all these curses** will come on you and overtake you: You will be cursed in the city and cursed in the country (...). (Deuteronomy 28: 15)

These laws have been established by God for the people of Israel, but apply to all those who wish to live a blessed life and avoid pitfalls. The Scriptures show us that breaking these laws can have terrible consequences on a person's or a nation's life.

- **The power of words**

"The tongue has the power of life and death, and those who love it will eat its fruit." (Proverbs 18:21)

The mouth has the power to bless, but also to curse. From the same mouth can proceed words of love, blessings and immediately after, words of hatred and condemnation: "With the tongue we **praise** our Lord and Father, and with it we **curse** human beings, who have been made in God's likeness." (James 3:9).

Words are very powerful. They can encourage, lift a person up, and push that person to do exploits, but words can also hurt and destroy. How many men and women become adults, broken by harsh words that were spoken to them when they were young? This does not bring a curse, I know, but it does leave traces etched deep in the person's heart. Damage caused by harsh words can be very painful and sometimes leave deeper aches than physical blows, even if neither is acceptable. Some words spoken over an individual's life can be weapons of mass destruction, depending on the content of the remarks (curses, incantations, spells, etc.)[2].

- **The practice of the occult**

The word occult is derived from the Latin word *occultus*, which means "secret, hidden". Occultism has always existed, but some of the practitioners are not always aware of the negative consequences it can have on their life and their families'. Clairvoyance, hypnosis, astrology, dowsing, shamanism, magic, witchcraft are all practices that have become very popular lately. Just look at how many websites offer such services. Yet, practicing occultism or consulting people who practice it can curse someone's life. Occultism includes all practices that consist of consulting

---

2. "Come, let us strike him with the tongue." (Jeremiah 18:18)

occult forces, communicating with the spirit world and the dead. Such practices are dangerous because when one attempts to communicate with a spirit other than the Spirit of God, they venture to communicate with evil and demonic spirits.

- **Musical inspiration**

Today, it is wise to carefully choose the type of music and artists you listen to, because it is known that some have chosen to ally with the Devil, in order to guarantee their success and fame.

Lately, the trend is that some artists don't even hide it anymore but rather openly speak about it.

Some songs have subliminal lyrics and some texts, when read or sung over and over, can cast spells on the listener, who is unconsciously repeating divinatory incantations. So, it is no coincidence that some popular musical circles are known for their marginal fans, in addition to a high suicide rate and heavy use of all kinds of drugs.

3 – How to end curses?

- **Generational curses**

Generational curses hang over a person, a family, or a nation, for one or more generations. The Bible teaches us that curses can follow up to four generations:

> He [God] maintaining love to thousands, and forgiving wickedness, rebellion and sin. Yet he does not leave the guilty unpunished; **he punishes the children and their children for the sin of the parents to the third and fourth generation!**" (Exodus 34:7)

It is important to always remember that as there are natural laws, there are spiritual laws as well. The transgression of some of these laws can lead to a curse. For instance, the law of sowing teaches us that every man harvests what he has sowed. It is an immutable law. He who sows love, harvests love, he who sows hatred, harvests hatred. Similarly, one who consults or works with evil spirits attracts misfortune, because of the exposure to the demonic world, and this can have repercussions on their loved ones.

But fortunately, when one becomes knowledgeable about these things, it is possible to get rid of them:

1. **Those who are victims of a demonic possession** (some voluntary or involuntary practices lead to demonic possession):

   - The first thing to do is to accept Jesus as personal Lord and Savior, by asking for forgiveness for your sins and for having practiced these occult practices for personal reasons or for your family, and repent.
   As already seen, this allows the Holy Spirit to come live in your heart. Then, you must surround yourself with people of strong faith, so that they walk with you and discern

the origin of the problem, thanks to the Holy Spirit. Depending on what comes to light, they will pray for your deliverance. You will of course have to put an end to these practices, by getting rid of books, objects and other items related to occultism.

It is important to know that it is dangerous to release someone who did not previously give their life to Jesus, because the Word of God teaches that if so, demons will come back more numerous and the person's condition will be worse than before. This is what Jesus taught His disciples:

> When an impure spirit comes out of a person, it goes through arid places seeking rest and does not find it. Then it says, 'I will return to the house I left.' When it arrives, it finds the house unoccupied, swept clean and put in order. **Then it goes and takes with it seven other spirits more wicked than itself, and they go in and live there. And the final condition of that person is worse than the first.** That is how it will be with this wicked generation. (Matthew 12:43-45)

2. Those who are victims of a curse

- If a person is cursed, due to their actions or their family's, they must ask God for forgiveness, repent for their sins or for their family's past deeds. Then this person must ask the Holy Spirit to reveal what kind of curse it is and destroy it in the name of Jesus: "Father, I thank you for having revealed this curse to me. I ask for your forgiveness and I repent of my deeds. I destroy this curse and I am now released from it in the name of Jesus." In some cases, it is better to ask for spiritually mature people's assistance.

In both cases, to remain delivered, one must:

- Close all the doors to the occult, sins and impurity.
- Walk in sanctification and obedience.

A very good friend gave her life to Jesus in December 2015. A few weeks later, she was joyfully baptized in the Holy Spirit. Unfortunately, some bad news came along with her joy. The doctors discovered that she had breast cancer. Barely 32, she was told it would be best to have both breasts removed, in order to avoid further complications. This news came as a terrible shock. She had got checked out because the doctors had noticed her mother was carrying a hereditary predisposing gene. Affected by the situation, a few brothers, sisters and I decided to pray for her health, believing that God was able to heal her. During the prayer periods, we asked several questions, in order to know exactly what to pray for, that is how we learned that her mother and four aunts were also carrying the gene. The Holy Spirit revealed us that it was actually a generational curse. This gene had mutated and was now affecting all the women of the family. We therefore asked her to inquire if her grandparents or members of the family had been involved in some occult practices in the past. After spending time with her mother, she learned that indeed, her grandparents from Madagascar had dabbled in witchcraft, besides someone angry with the family had cast a spell on them. Given she had given her life to Jesus, the generational curse could no longer impact her life, because Jesus had paid the price for her freedom and deliverance. The Bible is clear on this matter:

> Surely he took up our pain and bore our suffering, yet we considered him punished by God, stricken by him, and afflicted. But he was pierced for our transgressions, he was crushed for our iniquities; the punishment that brought us peace was on him, and by his wounds we are healed. (Isaiah 53:4-5)

She asked for God's forgiveness and repented for the secret occult practices of her grandparents. She also repented for some practices she was unaware of at the time. We then prayed to destroy all possible generational curse and it happened: the demonic spirits manifested. After ordering them to leave, we prayed for her recovery. She had a first MRI, which showed no cancer trace. She then had an ultrasound and a mammogram, which both confirmed the result of the MRI: she was healed. The cancer had disappeared. Her disease was associated with a generational curse which was hanging over the family.

Thus, the spiritual world is more real than some think and requires proper preparation, in order to fight the awaiting battles in one's life. Many fellow citizens suffer from various ailments that keep occurring in their lives and doctors never find any explanation to these diseases. Also, some patients who are admitted to psychiatric hospital as mentally insane, schizophrenic, or suicidal, are in reality subject to spiritual oppression or demonic possessions. A psychotherapist friend once told me that at the psychiatric hospital where she works, her colleagues and herself found one of their patients with slashed arms. She had written "the Devil is in me" on the bedroom's walls, with her own blood.

All social classes are concerned, including believers who gave their life to Jesus, but have not yet proceeded to this deliverance work, in order to be totally delivered from the bonds of the past. Whatever it is, Jesus came to set free and release all captive people. In His name, it is possible for any believer to totally and permanently be freed, thus turning the page on the past once and for all.

Chapter 2
From the trial by fire to victory

It is rare to encounter people who would say they enjoy hardship and difficulties. Yet, when we happen to talk with someone who went through difficult times, in hindsight they admit that through these tough times they have learned about their character and their relationship with God. God uses different ways to educate His children, bring them closer to His heart and uncover the treasures He has hidden or deposited in them. The desert and spiritual warfare are very special moments in the believer's life. Let us look at how God uses them to hone, perfect and strengthen His children.

1 – Victory in combat

Every weekend, parks and forests of Paris and its immediate surroundings are filled with joggers. Running is the most popular sport in France. Any runner who practices long distance knows that the most important is not the speed you begin at, but to rather finish the race. How many start at high speed and end up stopping midway? Some start again after catching their breath, while others completely give up and abandon the race. This image is a good illustration of the Christian life: it is a long-distance race. During that race, some moments are flat and easy, everything goes well, some slopes require no effort. There are hilly paths, with challenges and there are steep roads, where just one misstep makes one fall off the ravine.

The biggest challenge in Christian life is to hold on until the end. The Apostle Paul managed to hold on despite difficulties, imprisonments, beatings, stoning and criticism. He proudly declared at the end of his life: "I have fought the good fight, I have finished the race, I have kept the faith." (2 Timothy 4:7).

- **Faith, the battle of the believer**

Faith is the element that connects the believer to God. The Word of God defines faith as follows: "Now faith is confidence in what we hope for and assurance about what we do not see." (Hebrews 11:1). It also says that it is Jesus who arouses faith and leads it to perfection[1] and that without faith, it is impossible to please God[2]. Faith is like a seed planted in the heart of the believer, that develops gradually, as they maintain their communion with God, and grow through their personal experiences, which all demonstrate the divine intervention of the Father. One of the greatest challenges of the Devil is to sabotage the believer's faith, by attacking and causing them to doubt God's ability to look after them and intervene in their life. These attacks are designed to undermine convictions and beliefs, so the believer gives up and the doors of eternity remain closed. Unbelievers have a hard time apprehending those

---

1. Hebrews 12:2
2. Hebrews 11:6

concepts. For them, they simply live their lives, do no harm and cannot accept the fact that some of their behaviors can be associated with the Devil. However, as the day is opposed to the night, light against darkness, the Devil is opposed to God. These comparisons perfectly illustrate the fact that the Kingdom of God is diametrically opposed to the kingdom of Satan and that therefore, the one that is not within one necessarily ends up within the other. The Devil's attacks are triggered by the hatred he has for God. Having been dismissed from his angel-of-light position and ejected from heaven, he blames the creation of God and especially mankind. He projects evil thoughts against others or against himself, with the ultimate goal of destroying Creation.

- **Thoughts: the Devil's main targets of attack**

The Devil attacks the believer in various ways. It ranges from mind and thought oppression, diseases, occult practices (witchcraft, etc.), to specific situations that can destroy the believer physically, morally or even mentally. Yet, I wish to reassure you that as long as the believer follows the will of God, by walking in obedience and sanctification, the Devil cannot touch them. He has no legal right on the believer's life, as stated in this verse: "We know that anyone born of God does not continue to sin; the One who was born of God keeps them safe, and the evil one cannot harm them." (1 John 5:18). However, it may occur that God **allows** a difficult situation in your life, but if so, not only does He give you the ability to overcome the difficulty, but He uses it to teach you something and make you closer to His heart, or like He did for His servant job, to show the enemy that you remain faithful despite adversity.

> No temptation has overtaken you except what is common to mankind. And God is faithful; **he will not let you be tempted beyond what you can bear.** But when you are tempted, he will also provide a way out so that you can endure it. (1 Corinthians 10:13)

Mind and thought oppression being one of the main entry points of the enemy, we will focus on this topic, because it concerns every child of God with no exception, and prevents many from blooming spiritually and live the abundant life they are called for. His mode of operation is always the same. He infiltrates the believer's mind with negative thoughts, in such a subtle way that the believer thinks they are the one provoking these thoughts. When this happens, a battle begins between the believer's mind and their soul, because these thoughts are completely different from the believer's spiritual nature. Their spirit is holy, pure, regenerated and not at all affected by the enemy's wiles. But their soul or intellect, on the contrary, is constantly under attack and must handle it.

Being "spiritually dead", the non-believer does not experience this inner battle. They have no discernment between what comes from themselves and from the enemy, because their spirit has to be reborn in order to judge spiritual things.

Before going any further, one must understand how important it is to make the distinction between evil thoughts coming from man's heart, his carnal nature, passed injuries, personal problems, lack of confidence, difficult times he is going through and the thoughts that result from the enemy.

The field of mind and thought is so vast that it could be the topic of a book. What one must remember is that evil thoughts can come from three sources:

- **Oneself**
  - Scientists estimate that a human being has on average of 30,000 to 50,000 thoughts a day.
  - One's reasoning, education and culture.

- **The environment**
  - One's thoughts are influenced by their senses: hearing, smell, touch, sight and taste.
  - The things one looks at and hears on a regular basis eventually define their system of thought.

- **The soul's enemy**
  - The bad thoughts that come from the enemy.

The more the believer strengthens their spirit (through prayers, reading the Word of God, teachings, communion, fasting, etc.), the better they distinguish the thoughts coming from the enemy, among the thousands they have every day. What type of thought can come from the enemy? Thoughts that belittle, sadden, trigger fear and stress when there is no reason to be worried. But also, doubtful thoughts from one day to the other, when you question everything you have believed so far. Thoughts of anger, hatred, jealousy, grudge, suicide, moral impurity, sexual obsession or deviance, blasphemy, insults, etc.

- **Emotional consequences**

The purpose of his attacks is to discourage the believer and push them to let go and give up. These attacks can cause severe emotional damage and induce stress, worry, anguish, etc. in the life of the one undergoing them. These emotions can have effects on the body, like headaches due to stress, depression, illnesses, etc. In her book "Switch on my brain", Doctor Caroline Leaf explains that, according to a study conducted by the American Medical Association, 75% to 98% of mental illnesses result from a high level of worry. The same study states that stress is one of the main factors in 75% of illnesses people suffer from today[3].

- **The fight of faith in thoughts**

The Apostle Paul said: "For our struggle is not against flesh and blood, but against the rulers, against the authorities, against the powers of this dark world and against the spiritual forces of evil in the heavenly realms." (Ephesians 6:12). It is essential that the believer requests assistance from the Holy Spirit to discern, among their own thoughts, those that come from God and those that come from the enemy. The believer must reverse the old patterns of thought that led them to reproduce the same mistakes again and again and to believe the enemy's lies. That is why the Apostle Paul wrote to the inhabitants of Corinth, explaining the importance of aligning their thoughts on the mind of God. He told them:

---

3. Caroline Leaf: *Switch on my brain*, p.36

> The weapons we fight with are not the weapons of the world. On the contrary, they have divine power to demolish strongholds. We demolish arguments and every pretension that sets itself up against the knowledge of God, and **we take captive every thought to make it obedient to Christ**. (2 Corinthians 10:4-5)

When bad thoughts arise, we need to take authority and declare: "I refuse this thought." We then need to discipline ourselves and fix our attention on something else, to prevent that thought from troubling our peace. Whichever the battle the believer faces, they must never forget that they are not alone. God is by their side through His Holy Spirit. They must therefore strengthen both their faith and trust in the Word of God and meditate on passages that relate to their circumstances. The Word of God is the prime weapon to destroy the wiles of the enemy but to achieve so, one must know it and make it part of their daily life. Let us look at some verses that remind the believer of the presence of God by their side, in all circumstances:

> You, dear children, are from God and have overcome them, because the one who is in you is greater than the one who is in the world. (1 John 4:4)

He will also **keep you firm to the end**, so that you will be blameless on the day of our Lord Jesus Christ. (1 Corinthians 1:8)

Persecutions, sufferings I endured. **Yet the Lord rescued me from all of them.** (2 Timothy 3:11)

The Lord will rescue me from every evil attack and will bring me safely to his heavenly kingdom. To him be the glory for ever and ever. (2 Timothy 4:18)

I have given you authority to trample on snakes and scorpions and to overcome all the power of the enemy; **nothing will harm you.** (Luke 10:19)

No, in all these things we are **more than conquerors** through him who loved us. (Romans 8.37)

With God we will gain the victory, and **he will trample down our enemies.** (Psalms 108:14)

One day, a friend told me an African proverb: "If you never cross the Devil on your way, it is probably because he walks by your side". Every believer who wishes to do the will of their Father, will be confronted with adversity on their way, because the achievement of the Divine Will reveals His glory and the enemy will rebel against it. One must never get discouraged when the tempest begins to rage but rather keep walking, confident, because they are on the path of life.

2 – Victory in the desert

Each believer has their own story, their own encounter with God. Everyone is different, but they all have a common point, a turning point. Most can witness a "before and after". For some, this encounter took place at a time when they were questioning life in general, or at the time of a miraculous healing. For others, through a dream in which Jesus revealed Himself directly to them, or in hearing a poignant testimony from a friend or colleague. Finally, some have simply pushed the doors of a church and have been touched by the atmosphere and the love that reigned in the place.

Any person who has had a true encounter with Jesus can testify of it through the peace and joy they felt that day. A fire was kindled and passion was ignited in their heart. Yet, after a while, it felt as if the passion of the first days was getting weaker and weaker. While the person felt the presence of God by their side as they prayed, praised Him and enjoyed reading the Bible, going to church and gathering with brothers and sisters, it now feels like this "presence" is not as strong and, even in some cases, it seems to be gone. While the prayers were almost automatically answered, it now seems the answers are tardy.

Every Christian, at one point or another, goes through this stage. God very surely remains at the side of the believer, but He allows this "silence" to reveal Himself differently, to allow spiritual growth and increase the level of intimacy with Himself. To better illustrate this, let us look at the behavior of parents towards their new-born: when a child is just born, he receives his parents' entire attention and spends most of his time at their side or at least within sight.

Every baby, from birth, has an array of elementary sensory capacities that will develop throughout childhood and for this to happen, he has to progressively learn to do things on his own: hold his bottle, eat, become potty trained, etc. If at first his parents ran to his rescue when he cried and assisted him systematically with anything he needed, little by little they will allow him to do things on his own, so that he develops physical, sensorial and intellectual skills.

The same applies to God. Every newly converted person is affectionately called a "spiritual baby", because of the youth of their faith. Often, God meets their needs once the person prays, cries, manifests a need. But, as nature teaches us so well, it is necessary that after a while, babies become adults, autonomous and capable of standing on their own feet. God has placed great abilities inside each of His children but they must grow spiritually and become capable of using the gifts and talents He has deposited within them all, as each single one represents a facet of God Himself. He will therefore allow them to walk through the desert in order to teach, strengthen and perfect them.

- **The desert brings one closer the heart of God:**

    In 2012, I have personally experienced it. I recall that at the time, I had no idea of what I was going through. It is only much later, as I was accompanying a friend in a Christian bookstore in Paris, that I understood I was going through what is called the "spiritual desert". As I was walking through the alleys, I examined the hundreds of books in the hope of finding one that would help me understand my situation. After a while, not knowing which to choose, I whispered a quick prayer: "Lord, show me which book can help me. Amen." It seems that the shortest prayers are the best. Yet, while I hadn't heard anything special nor had any flash, I simply walked towards the books in the English language. As I was looking at the covers and titles, one caught my attention. It was entitled "Victory in the wilderness: Growing strong in dry times"[4] from John Bevere. When I got home, I began reading it and was amazed by the fact that the author was describing my present condition. The more I read, the more I understood what the desert and its purpose were. The author explained that when he was still a young pastor, he went through a desert experience that lasted 18 months. During that time, the relationship with his wife was tense and it allowed him to point at traits he needed to change, otherwise severe relationship problems would remain and deplete his spiritual growth. He later admitted that this transition period was necessary to break the things that, at some point in his life, would have prevented him from going any further with God and from accomplishing what God had planned for him. After the test, he came out of the desert, transformed, closer to

---

4. John Bevere: *Victory in the wilderness: Growing strong in Dry Times*, Ed. John Bevere Ministries, p. 171

God and freed from what could have dampened his growth. Today, he is a renowned writer who has written more than twenty books, many of which are best-sellers.

The following week, I went to my church and the pastor preached on... the desert! At the end of the service, a friend came to me and said she had received a word from God, in which she was told I was going through the desert but I shouldn't be afraid, because God allowed it in my life so I could achieve transformation. While she was speaking, I could read a bit of apprehension on her face because she needed me to confirm. This word was for me indeed: it was the third confirmation. In fact, the book you are now reading would have never existed, had I not experienced my desert time. From the time spent in the desert have come wonderful experiences, which have strengthened my faith, made my walk deeper rooted and caused me to reconsider my priorities and realign my will with that of the Most High.

You may have this question: "In which way does this draw you closer to God? "To understand, we need to draw a parallel between the physical desert and the spiritual one. In the same way that the extreme temperatures of the physical desert make you thirsty, similarly the spiritual desert pushes you to find something to ease your thirst. Only Jesus, who is the source of living water, can quench the thirst of the soul. That is why King David declared in one of the Psalms:

> You, God, are my God, earnestly I seek you; I thirst for you, my whole being longs for

you, in a dry and parched land where there is no water. (Psalm 63:2)

Jewellers put gold into the fire, in order to release any impurities and then work with it as they wish. In a passage from the Scriptures, the Apostle Peter compared the faith of the believer to gold purified by fire. He says:

> In all this you greatly rejoice, **though now for a little while you may have had to suffer grief in all kinds of trials. These have come so that the proven genuineness of your faith** - of greater worth than gold, which perishes even though refined by fire - may result in praise, glory and honor when Jesus Christ is revealed. (1 Peter 1:6)

The fire he speaks about reminds us of the extreme temperatures one encounters in the desert. The spiritual desert carves the character, shapes the identity, redefines the priorities and aligns them with God. God incites the believer to turn away from sin, to abandon bad habits, to put pride aside, to be aware of their bad temper, lack of love and of forgiveness.

Several characters in the Bible have gone through this experience before entering the fullness of their calling. Jesus was one of them. After He was baptized of water, the Spirit of God led Him through the desert where He fasted and prayed for 40 days. It is interesting to note that He was led by the Holy Spirit and not by the Devil. After this period, the Devil tried to tempt Him but He resisted. This separation allowed Him to prepare and agree with the Father, before He could begin His ministry on earth. When He left the desert, Jesus was equipped and fully ready to begin His mission: "Jesus returned to Galilee in the power of the Spirit, and news about him spread through the whole countryside." (Luke 4:14).

The same for the Apostle Paul, whose writings are renowned for their depth and their wealth. He had such a knowledge of the mysteries of God that even the Apostle Peter, when talking about him, said that certain points he addressed were "difficult to understand" and that "ignorant and not affirmed people would twist the meaning"[5]. The Apostle Paul spent three years in the desert of Arabia and it is likely that during that time of isolation, he received a large portion of revelations. The same for Moses and the people of Israel, who spent 40 years in the desert.

- **The desert allows the perfecting of the saints**

Place Vendôme is one of the wealthy international tourists' most famous landmarks in Paris. One can there find some of the finest stones and most beautiful jewels in the world. But before arriving there, most of these jewellery pieces undergo a real transformation process. For example, a diamond is formed from carbon that went through an extreme temperature of 1,200°C and underwent a pressure varying between 4.5 GPa[6] and 6 GPa, which corresponds to depths between 150 km and 1,000 km (approx. 95 to 620

---

5. 2 Peter 3:16
6. Symbol of the gigapascal, measurement unit of pressure of the international system.

miles) in the terrestrial coat[7]. Some diamonds such as the black diamond simply look like pieces of charcoal, when in their raw state. It is all the work done by the diamond worker and the merchant on the stone that will give it its worth. Diamond is the hardest natural material that exists. It can only be scratched or cut by another diamond. It is therefore after all this transformation that it will become a part of the most prestigious jewellers' collections. The name of this stone is derived from the ancient Greek word *Adàma*, which means "invincible, untameable, indestructible", as well as from *Adamastos*, which means "inflexible, **unwavering**". It is interesting to note that the Apostle Peter uses the same word *unwavering* in a passage that refers to the ability given by God to the believer to stand firm in the face of adversity. He says:

> And the God of all grace, who called you to his eternal glory in Christ, after **you have suffered** a little while, will himself **restore you** and **make you strong, firm and** steadfast. (1 Peter 5:10)

God made all things for a purpose. The reason Why God allows certain events in an individual's life is to forge, train and help that individual to defeat the attacks of the enemy and become a deliverer, for others who go through or will go through similar situations. The experience drawn from this situation enables the individual to help others. Very often, suffering and adversity are like fuel, in men and women of destiny's lives. Indeed, these sufferings push them to

---

7. From the Wikipedia website: https://en.wikipedia.org/wiki/Diamond (consulted on December 15, 2015).

discover their limits, solve and overcome these adversities. The tests and sufferings reveal their limits and draw them closer to the One who has no limits: God Himself.

- **What to do in this situation?**
    - **Have a good attitude.** The believer's attitude is very important. From the disposition of their heart will vary the duration of the desert experience, what they will (or will not) learn through this.

    - **Learn to draw lessons from it.** God uses the desert to change the believer's heart; it is therefore important that the believer questions themselves to understand the reason why God has allowed this desert experience in their life: "what does God wish to change in me?" My character, remove my pride, heal me of past injuries, test my faith and trust in Him, teach me to persevere… etc."

    - **Give up bad things.** Let God remove all impurities from the heart, even if it hurts. If they remain, they are an obstacle that prevents one from drawing closer to Him and represent a risk of relapsing into bad things.

    - **Learn how to decrease so that He increases.** Learn to silence and decrease the ego so that He increases and takes up more space in your heart. "He must become greater; I must become less." (John 3:30)

- **The benefits of the desert**

The desert forces one to slow down and take inventory of what is happening. This alone is already a significant exploit, amidst a society in which one is cornered by many activities. It forces one to put aside the futile and superficial and refocus on what is essential:

- Prayer, reading the Word and fasting
- Exercising one's faith
- The discovery of one's destiny
- The transformation of the inner being to make it unwavering
- Let God take control of one's life
- Learn not to rely on what is seen, but on what one believes

It is important to differentiate between the desert experience and spiritual warfare. **The desert is willed by God, whereas spiritual warfare is allowed by God.** In those two situations, God is always next to His child, even if the latter may feel all alone amidst their torment. Silence does not mean absence. Silence forces the child of God to draw closer to their father's heart and better learn to hear the Father's voice. It then becomes easier to develop a relationship with the Father, understand the challenges one goes through and draw lessons from them. Many times, the desert experience precedes a change in the believer's life and prepares them for it. Let us look at what destiny is.

FOURTH PART

Destiny

Chapter 1
From victory to destiny

I am convinced that these times are special times that God has chosen to reveal Himself to mankind in a special way. However, for this to happen, He needs His children to enter their destiny. Indeed, what better way to reveal what resides in you than by accomplishing what you were born for?

The Bible portrays several people that God chose for a special destiny: Abraham, Joseph, Moses, Joshua, Gideon, David, Jesus, Ruth, Esther, Mary and many others. The common characteristic is that the radical change within their life has benefited many others, their blessing having resulted in many others receiving blessings. Among them, a man, aged 17, had a dream about his destiny. His story is that of a young man used by God to save an entire nation.

1 – The fate of Joseph: a model of faithfulness

Joseph was the second last of twelve brothers and his father Jacob's favorite, which highly annoyed the others. One night, he had a dream he told them about, which only annoyed them further. He dreamed that his brothers and himself were tying sheaves in the middle of a field. In the dream, his sheaf was standing still while his brothers' were surrounding and bowing before it. Hearing this, his brothers were infuriated and asked him whether he honestly believed that he was going to rule over them. A few days later, he had a second dream he also told them about.

This time, he dreamed that the sun, the moon and the eleven stars were bowing before him. As they were listening, Joseph's brothers got angry and wanted to kill him, but one of them opposed such idea and suggested to throw him down a cistern instead, which they did. Days later, merchants who were heading to Egypt in a caravan drove past them. Joseph's brothers decided to sell him as a slave. The traders bought and sold him to Potiphar, Pharaoh's officer. Joseph therefore became Potiphar's servant and prospered the business of his master, who entrusted him everything he possessed because he could see the grace and favor of God within Joseph. But Joseph having become a handsome and great young man, Potiphar's wife attempted to seduce him on many occasions, so that he would sleep with her. When he refused, she continued to insist day after day and, offended by the resistance of the young man, she lied to her husband, saying Joseph had attempted to rape her. Enraged, Potiphar put him to jail. But the story of Joseph does not stop there. In prison, he met a cup-bearer or butler[1] and a baker[2]. During the night, both the butler and the baker had a dream they reported to Joseph, which he interpreted to them. Months later, the butler was freed and Joseph begged him to remember him when he would return to Pharaoh's court, but the butler forgot him. Two years later, Pharaoh had a dream and called all the magicians and wise men of

---

1. The cup-bearer was the one serving drinks to the King.
2. The baker used to prepare the King's bread.

Egypt to have it interpreted, but none of them could provide the meaning of the dream. The butler then remembered Joseph and spoke to Pharaoh. Pharaoh sent him to prison where the butler shared the dream with Joseph, who interpreted it. He explained that the country would know seven years of abundance, which would be followed by seven years of famine. Pharaoh had to choose a wise and intelligent man who could amass reserves during the seven years of abundance, to later deal with the seven years that would hit the country immediately after. In the face of Joseph's wisdom, Pharaoh chose him to accomplish this task, as showed in the following passage from the Scriptures:

> Then Pharaoh said to Joseph, "Since God has made all this known to you, there is no one so discerning and wise as you. You shall be in charge of my palace, and all my people are to submit to your orders. Only with respect to the throne will I be greater than you." So Pharaoh said to Joseph, "I hereby put you in charge of the whole land of Egypt." (Genesis 41:39-41)

As announced, the famine took place but the country handled the situation, thanks to the measures implemented by Joseph. The neighboring countries' inhabitants, knowing there was wheat in Egypt, came to provision themselves there and Jacob sent his sons, except Benjamin the youngest, who remained at his side. One day, Joseph, who was running the wheat sales, surprisingly saw men introducing and prostrating themselves before him. He recognized his brothers, who did not recognize him. He then remembered the first dream he had when he was younger. Without revealing his identity, he asked them to come back with their youngest brother. He kept one of them captive to make sure they would come back. The brothers came back with the youngest, but they still did not recognize him. After a while, Joseph ended up revealing his identity to them. Right away, his brothers feared that he would take revenge for their bad actions towards him. But he reassured them, saying:

> And now, do not be distressed and do not be angry with yourselves for selling me here, because it was to save lives that God sent me ahead of you. For two years now there has been famine in the land, and for the next five years there will be no ploughing and reaping. But God sent me ahead of you to preserve for you a remnant on earth and to save your lives by a great deliverance. **So then, it was not you who sent me here, but God. He made me father to Pharaoh, lord of his entire household and ruler of all Egypt.** (Genesis 45:5-8)

The brothers returned to find their father Jacob and took refuge in Egypt with the rest of the family, to escape the famine. Joseph's two dreams became true after seventeen years.

Through those two dreams, one understands that God had predestined Joseph to become the second person in charge of Egypt, to rescue his people from the famine that would hit. When Pharaoh had the dream and consulted his whole entourage, it turned out that Joseph alone was able to provide the interpretation. It is through the gift of interpretation given by God that he could explain the butler's and then Pharaoh's dreams. In fact, the revelation and the interpretation both came from God.

The gift of a man leads him to his destiny when he remains faithfully connected to the one who has granted the gift. Joseph remained faithful to God despite all the events he had gone through. At no point was he angry or even revolted against God. But the gift is not enough, it must be exercised. And it is in exercising the gift that Joseph had access to Pharaoh. The dream of the latter was an opportunity provided by God so he could get closer to power. His gift was the key that allowed him to cross the royal palace's gate. This should remind us of King Solomon's proverb that says: "Do you see someone skilled in their work? They will serve before kings; they will not serve before officials of low rank." (Proverbs 22:9). Joseph successfully executed his mission because he remained **loyal** and **faithful** against all odds. This is what allowed the grace and favor of God to always remain in his life.

Thus, he went from the status of prisoner to that of prime Minister of a Kingdom, in no time. Pharaoh could have simply released and covered him in wealth, but he rather made him his right-hand man. Joseph ignored it at the time, but he was evolving throughout his destiny and as a result, the circumstances and the decisions of men converged all in his favor, because they were perfectly aligned with the will of God. This is why, despite the many twists and negative circumstances along the way, he nevertheless ended up achieving the goal God had designed for him. His destiny was utmost importance, since God used it to ensure Egypt's economic stability and above all, the survival of Jacob and his family, which was the future of the nation of Israel. We need to be reminded that God had changed Jacob's name into Israel and from his descendants, the nation of Israel was born. In saving Jacob and his family, Joseph saved the destiny of a nation, the people of Israel. In protecting Jacob, God honored the covenant he made with Abraham, Jacob's great-grandfather, with Isaac and Jacob himself, a few years earlier.

2 – What do we learn from this story?

From a superficial point of view, it is just a story with a happy ending. But if we take time to look deeper, we can only be astonished by how the negative situations in Joseph's life have all come to work in his favor. His life is rich in teachings, there is much that could be said and there are two significant points I wish to underline:

- Joseph was born for a very specific purpose.
- The choices and the decisions he had to make impacted not just his life but also others'.

Without knowing it, Joseph progressed according to a divine script, written before his time and it is only later that he understood it all. The dreams he had as a teenager turned out to be a projection of his future, an image of his destiny.

Whenever I have the opportunity to talk about destiny, I realize that many people ignore how important destiny is and by the end of our conversation, these people usually ask themselves if their lives were destined to a specific purpose or whether this is reserved to a specific group of people only. It is true that our perception of destiny always relates to men and women who have accomplished great things and marked history in a positive manner. Most of us admire these people to a certain extent. Just look at how popular their biographies or autobiographies are, whether books or films. Yet, destiny is not reserved to a special group of people. Destiny concerns each and every man. Reaching our destiny is written in our DNA. God the Son Himself, having become a man in order to save mankind, accomplished His purpose on earth. Let us look at His destiny and how He accomplished it.

3 – Jesus: a perfect model of destiny

Jesus came to earth with a purpose: **reveal the Father and save humanity**. He was conceived in the womb of a virgin, by the power of the Holy Spirit, which made Him a pure and sinless man. A specific episode occurred in His life while He was only 12. This event reveals that despite His young age, He was aware of His mission.

- **Jesus knew His destiny from the age of 12**

After celebrating the Passover in Jerusalem like every year, His parents returned to Nazareth, several days of walk away[3]. Jesus was not at their sides, but they were not worried: they simply thought He was with travelling companions, relatives or family acquaintances. But having walked a whole day without seeing Him, they came to think He had remained in Jerusalem. So, they decided to turn back and found Him sitting in the temple, discussing with the doctors of the Law. The doctors were surprised by the questions and the knowledge of this young boy. When His parents saw Him, they could not help but reprimand Him because they were worried. However, Jesus said something very surprising, for a child of this age. He said to them: "Why were you looking for me? Did you not know that I must be doing the works of my Father?" (Luke 2:49). Jesus already knew why He was on earth.

- **Jesus announces His entry into His destiny**

Although He knew the reasons for His coming to earth, He did not begin His ministry before being baptized in water and in the Spirit. The day of His baptism, the sky opened and the Holy Spirit descended upon Him in the form of a dove, and a voice was heard from heaven: "You are my beloved son, in you I have put all my affection." (Luke 3:22). He was 30 years of age. Immediately after, the Spirit of God led Him into the wilderness, where He fasted and prayed for 40 days. During that period, the Father and Himself spoke to prepare that to which He had been called. This stage was necessary to complete His destiny. During

---

3. Luke 2: 41-49.

this time of being set apart, the Devil came to test Him on several occasions but Jesus never gave in and resisted until the end. The Scriptures tell us that when He left the desert, He was clothed in the power of the Holy Spirit and equipped to begin His ministry. Immediately, He made the reason for His coming known. He entered the synagogue, where He was handed the book of the Prophet Isaiah and He read the following passage in front of the assembly, as an inaugural address:

> The Spirit of the Lord is on me, because he has anointed me to proclaim good news to the poor. He has sent me to proclaim freedom for the prisoners and recovery of sight for the blind to set the oppressed free, to proclaim the year of the Lord's favor. (Luke 4:18-19)

The rest of the text tells us:

> Then he rolled up the scroll, gave it back to the attendant and sat down. The eyes of everyone in the synagogue were fastened on him. He began by saying to them, **"Today this scripture is fulfilled in your hearing."** (Luke 4:21)

When Jesus began His Ministry, His intentions were clear: **to reveal the Father**. Nobody else but Him was better placed to talk about God, because no one knew the Father as much as He did. That is what He actually told

Philip, one of His disciples, when Philip asked: "Lord, show us the Father and that will be enough for us." (John 14:8). Jesus replied:

> Don't you know me, Philip, even after I have been among you such a long time? **Anyone who has seen me has seen the Father**. How can you say, 'Show us the Father'? Don't you believe that I am in the Father, and that the Father is in me? The words I say to you I do not speak on my own authority. Rather, it is the Father, living in me, who is doing his work. Believe me when I say that I am in the Father and the Father is in me; or at least believe on the evidence of the works themselves. (John 14:9-11)

His Ministry on earth lasted only three and a half years, but during that short time He performed signs and wonders that no one had done before Him. He restored the broken hearts, taught on the kingdom of God, healed the sick, cast out demons, rose men from the dead, walked on water, changed water into wine, multiplied food, calmed the storm and did many other extraordinary things as evidenced by the Bible itself: "Jesus did many other things, if they were to be all written in detail, the world could not contain the books that would be written." (John 21:25).

- **Jesus accomplishes His mission**

One day, Jesus and three of His disciples, Peter, James and John, set themselves apart on a high mountain. A few days earlier, He had promised that some of them would not die before seeing the kingdom of God come in all its power. As they were on the mountain, a supernatural event occurred:

> There he was transfigured before them. His face shone like the sun, and his clothes became as white as the light. Just then there appeared before them Moses and Elijah, talking with Jesus. Peter said to Jesus, "Lord, it is good for us to be here. If you wish, I will put up three shelters - one for you, one for Moses and one for Elijah." While he was still speaking, a bright cloud covered them, and a voice from the cloud said, "This is my Son, whom I love; with him I am well pleased. Listen to him!" (Matthew 17:2-5)

The transfiguration announced the coming glory of Jesus as the Son of God. This representation of Himself in the future revealed His glory to the disciples who were present. The Son of God came to save mankind. The Bible says:" He came not to be served, but to serve[4]. His entire life was motivated by His love for His father and for mankind. He explained this to His disciples:

> The reason my Father loves me is that I lay down my life - only to take it up again. No one takes it from me, but I lay it down of my own accord. I have authority to lay it down and authority to take it up again. This command I received from my Father. (John 10:17, 18)

The purpose of His life was to serve His Father, by offering His life as the perfect sacrifice, in order to take the award that weighed on all of humanity, and thus liberate the creation from eternal death. When Jesus died on the cross, the Devil thought he had defeated Him, while in reality, unknowingly He had served God's interests by crucifying His Son. Having committed no sin during His earthly life, death could not hold the Messiah back. On the third day, Jesus rose from the dead and walked out of the tomb. The world of darkness, principalities, dominions and authorities in heavenly places trembled with fright when they saw Him, because at that very moment they all understood that they were defeated. Furthermore, a few days before His crucifixion, Jesus told His Father something that should engage every believer: "[Father], **I have glorified you on earth, I have finished the work you gave me to do**." (John 17:4). If He could make this declaration in all confidence, it is because He knew without a doubt what the

---

[4]. "Just as the Son of Man did not come to be served, but to serve, and to give his life as a ransom for many." (Matthew 20:28).

purpose of His life was. This mission motivated His coming to earth, determined the choosing of the apostles He kept by His side, and **was successful** thanks to His cooperation and obedience to the Father. Jesus was so passionate about His doings that one day He told His disciples, who were rushing Him to eat: "My food is to do the will of the One who sent me and to complete His work." (Jn. 4:34). His joy was to accomplish the perfect will of His Father.

Everyone was wondering by what power He managed to accomplish all these miracles. One day, He revealed "His secret":

> Very truly I tell you, the Son can do nothing by himself; he can do only what he sees his Father doing, because whatever the Father does the Son also does. (John 5:19)

The secret of His success resides in the fact that He took no initiative on His own, but He was perfectly in accordance with the will of the Father. That is why all His requests found a favorable response. Jesus was chosen for a special mission: reveal the Father and save the creation from the yoke of the Devil. The anointing of the Holy Spirit was the power by which He operated, to accomplish this special mission and act in the supernatural. He came to introduce a perfect lifestyle according to God: do His will. Those who also wish, by the end of their life, to state: "It is accomplished", must imperatively **discover the purpose of their creation** and **do the will of God**. Thus, the Father will be glorified and their existence on earth will have purpose.

- **Jesus: pioneer of a people's destiny**

Jesus could only accomplish miracles because He was perfectly united with the Father and because He allowed the power of the Holy Spirit to act in Him and through Him. The disciples were amazed by His knowledge, His power and His miracles. Yet, one day, He told them:

> Very truly I tell you, **whoever believes in me will do the works I have been doing, and they will do even greater things than these**, because I am going to the Father. And I will do whatever you ask in my name, so that the Father may be glorified in the Son. You may ask me for anything in my name, and I will do it. (John 14:12-14)

How could the disciples achieve the things Jesus did?

By the power of the Holy Spirit. Indeed, if we carefully look at His journey, we can see that Jesus began His Ministry the day when the power of the Holy Spirit came down on Him. And just before leaving them, He made a promise:

> **But you will receive power when the Holy Spirit comes on you**; and you will be my witnesses in Jerusalem, and in all Judea and Samaria, and to the ends of the Earth. (Acts 1:8)

The Greek word for power is *dunamis*, which later formed the root of the words **dynamic** and **dynamite**: The power of the Holy Spirit in a believer makes them dynamic and turns them into dynamite.

As promised, the Apostles Peter, Paul, John and the others received the power of the Holy Spirit and they accomplished extraordinary things that marked the beginnings of the Church and Christianity. The Acts of the Apostles recounts how the Holy Spirit was actively close to the disciples, accompanying each during the mission that was entrusted to them. The Holy Spirit was the main actor, the main intermediary between heaven and earth. The Holy Spirit is still present and more than ever willing to manifest the person of Jesus on earth, by clothing the people of God with His power. That is also what the Prophet Joel prophesied in his time: "After that, I will pour out my spirit on all human being; your sons and your daughters will prophesy, your old people will have dreams, and your young people will have visions." (Joel 3:1).

4 – Make visible what is hidden

The people of God has been commissioned to make God visible on earth, revealing the divine nature that resides in Him. The Bible says: "For the creation waits in eager expectation for the children of God to be revealed."(Romans 8:19). The original Greek word used in this passage for revelation is *apokalupsis*, which means "use of events, by which things or the nature of some, hidden so far, become visible to all". A revelation therefore makes something that already existed visible, but that was invisible to the eyes of men thus far.

In order to unfold and reveal the glory of God, His people must acquire sufficient spiritual maturity to become conscious of His identity in Christ and aware of the power of the Holy Spirit that acts in each one of them. So many children of God miss the impactful and influential life they have been called to, because they are not aware of their identity.

At the beginning of His Ministry, Jesus taught His disciples, explaining they were the salt of the Earth and the light of the world[5]. The image of salt represents flavor, the taste a Christian must bring to their environment, family, workplace, demonstrating the fruit of the Spirit. As for the light, it symbolizes enlightening those who are lost and seeking true light. Imagine a poor man, with no money, who only owns the house he lives in, which he has inherited from his parents. On one of the living room's walls, there is a painting worth millions of euros, which he ignores, though. He will live his whole life in poverty without ever realizing that the solution to his problems is right there in front of his eyes. Unfortunately, many Christians are just like him, unaware of the inheritance God has left them and of the ability they have to enlighten the world. They live a life below the standard of the one they have been called to, simply because they are not aware of their divine nature. Yet, creation, including your entourage and all the people your destiny will impact in one way or another, eagerly awaits your revelation. In other words, that you reveal what is in you because maybe you have the answer to their questions, the solution to their problems. Let us look at this legacy.

---

5. Matthew 5:13-14

This legacy contains[6]:

- **An authority:** the name of Jesus

    > Very truly I tell you, my Father will give you whatever you ask in my name. Until now you have not asked for anything in my name. Ask and you will receive, and your joy will be complete. (John 16:23-24)

- **A mandate:** proclaim the name of Jesus to the whole world.

    > Therefore go and make disciples of all nations, baptizing them in the name of the Father and of the Son and of the Holy Spirit, and teaching them to obey everything I have commanded you. And surely I am with you always, to the very end of the age. (Matthew 28: 19-20)

- **A weapon:** the Word of God

    > For the Word of God is alive and active. Sharper than any double-edged sword, it

---

6. Franck Lefillatre: message preached at the Paris Metropole Church on May 19, 2013, on the website of « L'Église Paris Metropole »: https://www.monegliseparis.fr/sermon/S%C3%A9rie-la-r%C3%A9v%C3%A9lation-des-fils-de-dieu-1 (consulted on October 15, 2015).

> penetrates even to dividing soul and spirit, joints and marrow; it judges the thoughts and attitudes of the heart. (Hebrews 4:12)

- **A Power:** the Holy Spirit

> But you will receive power when the Holy Spirit comes on you; and you will be my witnesses in Jerusalem, and in all Judea and Samaria, and to the ends of the Earth. (Acts 1:8)

It also implies rights and duties:

▶ **Rights:**

- An unmerited grace: the salvation of the soul, eternal life

- The authority of the name of Jesus. Jesus said to His disciples: "Behold, I have given you the power to walk on snakes and scorpions, and over all the power of the enemy; and nothing will harm you" (Luke 10:19).

- The protection of God

- The power of the Holy Spirit

- The prayer: "And whatsoever you ask in my name, I will do, that the Father may be glorified by the Son." (John 14:13)

These rights are directly attributed to one who accepts God in their life.

▶ **Duties:**

- Obedience
- Sanctification
- The walk by faith
- The fear of the Lord
- Doing the will of God

When men and women become aware of their identity in Christ, they realize they have rights and duties they need to honor, if they want to fulfill their destiny. In refusing, the believer moves away from God's plans for their life and from God Himself.

Chapter 2
D.E.S.T.I.N.Y

1 – Everyone has their own story

"All the days ordained for me were written in your book before one of them came to be." (Psalm 139:16). The author of life wrote a wonderful book with your name as title. This book is like none else because it contains a unique story, which has specifically been written just for you. It must be achieved in this present time, in this generation, because it contributes to a large number of other stories. Thus, your story is intertwined in others' and contains pieces of the puzzle, that have to be gathered to design a gigantic fresco. This fresco is a masterpiece designed to catch the eye towards its Designer. That is why, like any other creation bearing the signature of its designer, you carry the signature of your author.

During your earthly pilgrimage, you can never live a more beautiful story than the one written just for you, because your entire being has been shaped around it. By giving life to each word, line, chapter, event, encounter, element that makes your story, you will live fully. Your character, your ethnic origin, your culture, your family environment, your talents and everything that defines your identity have nothing to do with chance. They all are in perfect harmony with God's plan for your life.

But it is up to you to discover and fulfill it. To this end, you must come closer to the Author of your story, because nothing is automatic. God gives everyone freedom of will to live the story He has written for them, or not. Your decision will determine the story you live: the one written by God or the one you will choose to live.... Indeed, our days are counted and set by God, but the pages of our life's book are virgin and every morning we write them through the choices we make.

Once a year, two major festivals take place: one in Cannes, France, and the other in the United States - the Golden Globe Awards that reward the best films of the year. During these ceremonies, the best director and the best actor are awarded a prize for their work. Whenever an actor receives a prize, they almost systematically thank the film director, because they understand they were able to give the best of themselves thanks to the script and the role assigned to them. Without denying the hard work put in, the actors know that the end result has to do with the director's instructions and the fact that he guided them throughout the script. Collaboration and good understanding between the director and the actor contribute to the film's success. These elements are totally invisible to the eyes of the beholder, but they remain the key ingredients to film success.

2 – Everyone has their own destiny

Discovery

Emerge

Significance

Trajectory

Influence

Nature

Yes

Your **DESTINY** consists of giving life to the story the Creator has written for you in heaven. Its **DISCOVERY** allows you to better understand the person you are, to **EMERGE** and shine like a star. It gives **SIGNIFICANCE** to your existence, by drawing the perfect **TRAJECTORY** you need to follow to succeed and change the world around you, by making it better. It **INFLUENCES** others, in giving them the desire to refuse a normal life, by welcoming their own story and original **NATURE** with a **"YES"**.

3 – Knowing who "I am", to know "where I'm going"

Most of you know the story of Moses and how God chose him to free his people who were enslaved in Egypt for 40 years. One day, as he was grazing his father-in-law Jethro's herd, the Angel of the Lord appeared and told him:

> I have indeed seen the misery of my people in Egypt. I have heard them crying out because of their slave drivers,

and I am concerned about their suffering. So I have come down to rescue them from the hand of the Egyptians and to bring them up out of that land into a good and spacious land, a land flowing with milk and honey (…). (Exodus 3:7-8)

Moses replied: "**Who am I**, to go to Pharaoh, and to lead the children of Israel out of Egypt?" (Exodus 3:11). Moses could not understand that God had chosen him for this mission, because he was feeling completely unable to accomplish it. The image he had of himself was altered by his weaknesses, inabilities and failures. He used to see himself as a simple shepherd, a herdsman, while God was seeing him as a leader, a liberator. In order to achieve what God was asking him, he first had to understand and accept the way God was seeing him. He needed to become aware of his ability to perform the given task, knowing he could rely on the help of God. God had called him because he knew what had been placed in him. Indeed, the Bible tells us: "The LORD does not look at the things people look at. People look at the outward appearance, but the LORD looks at the heart."(1 Samuel 16:7).

When looking at the different characters of the Bible, we notice that **whenever God chooses someone to accomplish a particular mission, He first reveals how He sees them**, that is to say that He first reveals the individual's true identity. The one He gave them when He created them, not the one from their parents, friends, circumstances or past. We have the example of Abraham, the patriarch. When God announced what He had chosen for him, He said: "We no longer shall call you Abram; but your name will be called Abraham because I make you the father of many nations."

(Genesis 17:5). The name God gave him was matching his new identity. A new identity, according to the way God was seeing him, not according to how men were seeing him. The same with Gideon. When God showed up in front of him, He called him "valiant hero", while he and his people were suffering oppression from the Midianites. God was seeing him as a warlord, a warrior capable of destroying his oppressor, while he certainly was not seeing himself as such: "Ah my Lord, how will I deliver Israel? Behold, my family is poor in Manasseh, and I am the smallest in the house of my father." (Judges 6:15). The same with David. God chose to make him king after Saul, while he was just a simple 17-year-old shepherd[1]. Besides, I am convinced that it is because David knew he was destined to be king, that he found the strength and boldness to go fight the giant Goliath[2]. He knew God was with him, because he agreed to see himself as God was seeing him (a king), which very certainly gave him additional force.

Maybe you, like Moses, Gideon and many others, feel completely unable to accomplish what God has planned for you. Whatever the mission He has projected for you, do not be worried but rather trust Him completely, because it is Him who makes you capable. As one of my friends often says: **"God does not call qualified people but He sure qualifies those He calls".** However, in order to be sure about your calling: you must first understand and accept your identity as son or daughter of God. As soon as you

---

1. I Samuel 16 :12
2. The story of David and Goliath is told in the first Book of Samuel: "The people of God is at war against the Philistines. As the two armies are facing each other, Goliath, a Philistine three-meter-high giant comes every day to insult the adverse army. Everyone is afraid to fight against him, except David who kills him with the help of a simple sling" (1 Samuel 17).

accept it, you will see yourself as He sees you and you will become aware of who you are in Christ. This simple acceptance opens the doors to your destiny.

As seen in the third chapter, God created Man in His image, His likeness. The Bible says: "Then God said: "Let us make mankind in our image, **in our likeness**, (…).""

God created mankind in His own image, in the image of God He created them; male and female He created them. (Genesis 1:26-27). In this passage, the original word used in Hebrew for image is *tselem*. *Tselem* means "image", but it also means "shadow". In the beginning, men were created as the shadow of God. Although sin came to tarnish this original identity, God wanted men to return to their original image, before the fall of Adam and Eve. For this, men must discover their identity in God, by getting closer to the source again, in order to fully reflect it and thus become the shadow of God again. The further we stand from God, the less we resemble Him, therefore the less we receive God's light and life. The closer we get to God, the more we discover who we are in God. It is in this intimacy that one will, just like Moses, ask God **"Who Am I?"** It is only when one understands who they are that they will also understand what they have been destined to.

When one discovers who is calling, they discover their call and it is then that the Holy Spirit reveals the story residing within themselves. One cannot go without the other.

4 – Destiny: a divine seed

The Bible tells us that three days after creating the world, God said:

> **"Let the land produce** vegetation: seed-bearing plants and trees on the land that bear fruit with **seed** in it, according to their various kinds." And it was so. The land produced vegetation: **plants bearing seed according to their kinds and trees bearing fruit with seed in it according to their kinds.** (Genesis 1:11-12)

It is first in the soil that God dropped **seeds** and ordered them to produce seeds in turn. Then the sixth day, **He created Man from the Earth.** The Bible says:

> Then the Lord God formed a man from the dust of the ground and breathed into his nostrils the breath of life, and the man became a living being. (Genesis 2:7)

Coming from the Earth, Man carries within himself the seeds that God had spread there at the time of Creation. Like the Earth, Man has the capacity to also produce life, to bear fruit. It is engraved in him. Nature proves to us that there cannot be life without an original seed. Thus, any person who gives life, whether to a newborn or to the dreams and projects God has written in their heart, answers the original order given by God: "be fruitful" (Genesis 1:28).

In other words: "Give life to the seeds I have placed in you". **Some seeds give human life and others produce divine life.**

- **Similarity between Man and the Earth**

It is interesting to observe that there is a very strong connection between Man and the Earth. Indeed, when looking at the necessary ingredients for quality fruit, we see that **good soil**, sufficient **water** and **sun** are mandatory. Otherwise, it is impossible for the seeds to germinate: they all end up stifling and die. It is the same for Man. For him to give life to the dreams God has placed within his heart, the following ingredients are needed:

- Good soil, which is like a healthy heart.
- Rain: the rain of the Holy Spirit to lead, inspire and make Man capable.
- Sun: Jesus, the light of the world, is the One showing the way one should follow.

5 – Characteristics of destiny

- **Destiny is a journey**

Destiny is the awareness of an innate destination in you, a place where you must go. It is a place where God wants to lead you and reveal Himself in a special way, in you and through you. It is an adventure that turns the traveller into an explorer of life, of God, of themselves, and of the world that surrounds them. During this journey, the most important is not only the destination but the way to reach it. Each step brings you closer to the heart of God and enables you to discover and know Him intimately. It also allows you to liberate the treasures that have been deposited in you and help others benefit from them.

The vision of the destination helps you make the right decisions and choices to get there. The sooner this discovery, the better for you, because you will soon be pretty able to make some valuable choices and decisions. In case you do not know how yet, do not worry: we will see in the next chapter how to find this destination. But one thing is sure: you will never have a complete and detailed vision of your trip. The Holy Spirit draws the road map and defines the steps, then you need to be attentive in order to follow his leadership. In fact, you will see that in some cases, it is even better not to be given all the details, otherwise you could end up discouraged before even starting. Remember the story of Joseph and of King David: At the age of 17, the first had dreams and the second was anointed to be king. Yet, 13 years went by before any of them could begin to see the manifestation of what they had received and during all these years, their lives were everything but a long and quiet river. But with hindsight, we see that the process had prepared them to later bear high duties which became theirs.

A comparison can be made with old hot air balloons. Indeed, the pilots used to lighten the nacelle by throwing the sand bags overboard, in order to gain altitude. The lighter the basket, the higher the hot air balloon could arise and soar. To reach your destination, you will have to throw some sand bags overboard, those that prevent you from taking height. For some, it might be a matter of turning the page on a painful past, for others a lack of confidence, for others the setting aside of pride or for others deciding to forsake some friendships, etc. You will have to learn not to depend on your own strength, but rather on the fire the Holy Spirit will blow in your sails, just like the blower in the hot air balloon, to help you take heights towards a new dimension.

By the end of the trip, you will no longer be the same person. The transformation is such that it is possible to distinguish a person who fulfills their destiny from one who is not at all fulfilling theirs. The one who walks in their calling is passionate about what they do, communicates their zeal and passion to those who surround them. This person is connected to Jesus, because they know that without Him they can do nothing: "If you remain in me and I in you, you will bear much fruit; apart from me you can do nothing." (John 15:5). This person is now aware that their life participates in the fulfillment of a much larger plan, one that is bigger than the person themselves, a divine plan.

- **Destiny gives meaning to your life**

Destiny is the most beautiful journey, it is like a sweet-smelling perfume, it gives savor to life, **it is the salt of life.**

Salt has several functions:

- It gives taste to food
- It preserves food
- It melts the ice on roads in winter

These three characteristics of salt give us a picture of what destiny is able to produce in your life.

- Destiny gives **taste, flavor** to your life. Your life becomes exciting.

- Destiny prevents you from allowing the gifts and talents God has placed within you from **rotting**. You will use, expand and develop them to their fullest potential.

- Destiny **melts** obstacles and difficulties of life away. Each of your steps is safe because you walk on the path that has been prepared for you. This does not mean you will encounter no difficulties, but the trials and circumstances that God will allow will contribute to your development and therefore to your destiny. Every time you overcome a difficulty, you will get closer to the goal, just like Joseph. The trials he went through enabled him to grow. Living what you have been called to fills you with passion and an ability to keep moving forward, even when everything seems to be going bad.

- Destiny: the real projection of you in Christ

When God calls you, He no longer looks at what you were, but He sees the person He called you to be, and what He has deposited in you. The Bible tells us: ''If anyone is in Christ, he is a new creature; old things are past; behold all things are become new.'' (2 Corinthians 5:17). That is why, when God reveals your destiny to you, you may think it is destined to someone else: it looks so unrealistic and implausible. Some people even believe this cannot be destined to them, because they look at themselves, their limits and their disabilities, while God sees them otherwise.

Chapter 3
Discover your destiny

1 – Everyone dreams

From the beaches of Dakar, Senegal, where very early in the morning young boys practice Senegalese wrestling in hope of becoming the next national hero, to Moscow, where for long hours, boys and girls rehearse classical ballet with the greatest teachers in the world, or to Paris, the capital of gastronomy, where amateur and professional cooks come to hone their skills in hope of becoming worldwide recognized chefs... everyone has a dream, deep within their heart. Coach Tony Stoltzfus said:

> Dreams are powerful. Dreams and the ones who dream them can change cultures, redirect nations and move mountains. Dreams bring life to hearts with a passionate energy and lead us to action and provide us with hope that a better future is not only possible, but

imperative. Dreams are images of our passions projected in the future[1].

Among the multitude of dreams you may have, there is one that stands out. One that makes your heart beat in a very particular way. One that is anchored in you because it corresponds to your true story, the one that was written in you by the Creator, even before you were born.

The story God has written for you might be shaped like a dream rooted in you forever. Around that dream, many smaller dreams revolve, like steps to bring you closer to Him, and each step changes you, and this change prepares you and makes you able to fulfill the next dream of your life.

You will never succeed if you are not transformed to the size of your dream. God's dream for your life is that you become the person He has created. This transformation takes place as you give life to the dreams He has deposited in you, which will bring change in you, in the lives of your loved ones, and some may even change the world. Every person who fulfilled their dream had to be transformed to accomplish so, whether politicians, athletes, business managers, artists or experts in any field. On several occasions, the Scriptures underline this transformation. In the case of Jesus for example, the Bible tells us: "He grew and fortified himself"[2] and regarding the Apostle Paul: "He fortified himself everyday a bit more"[3]. These simple indications

---

1. Tony Stoltzfus: *Christian Life Coaching Handbook: Calling and Destiny Discovery Tools for the Christian Life Coaching*, Ed. Coach 22 Bookstore LLC, USA, p. 124.
2. Luke 2: 40
3. Acts 9: 22

allow us to understand that they both have been transformed to accomplish their mission entrusted by the Father. Likewise, **you will have to be transformed to meet the expectations of your ambitions.**

2 – The dreams of God for your life

"A dream is an inspiring picture of the future that energizes your mind, will, and emotions, empowering you to do everything you can to achieve it." John Maxwell.

- **Dreams from sleep**

Just like Joseph, who on two occasions had a dream, your destiny may be revealed to you through one or several dreams. The dream is a means through which God manifests His will or reveals the future, in order to enlighten a person[4].

Whenever this dream comes back, there is a special resonance in you because it corresponds to what you have been called to accomplish. It distinguishes itself from other dreams, just because the mere thought of it awakens zeal and passion in you. It can be the little boy who keeps dreaming he is a fireman saving lives, to the little girl seeing herself opening an orphanage to help children. These dreams will keep reoccurring throughout their lives. These are not just childhood dreams that change and evolve according to the age, but are indeed the stories of their lives. Once they become adults, you will see them make these dreams come

---

4. From the website of "The Catholic Church of France": http://www.eglise.catholique.fr/glossaire/songe/ (consulted on March 16, 2016).

true. And those who don't fulfill their dreams will express some sort of frustration for not having achieved what mattered most to them. Fortunately, it is never too late to begin.

- **Dreams rooted in you**

Know that often, the dreams you have in the bottom of your heart that keep coming back are dreams that God has placed in you, which He wants you to fulfill, because they have the power to bring change and reveal God Himself. It is true that sometimes, some can doubt, because their dream seems far behind the traditional and religious idea they have of God. It is important not to put God "in a box". The Word tells that all things were made by Him and for Him[5]. He has inspired arts, music, singing, dancing, medicine, business, construction, innovation, languages and all possible human disciplines. And it is not because some people have diverted or perverted some initially good things that one should reject them and say they do not come from God.

However, it is also possible that some of your dreams do not come from God. In order to make sure you are in His will, you need to have discernment, to sift your dreams with the Word of God, to look at what motivates the dream, whether its aim is to serve God or for personal glory only, and to pray to distinguish which dreams are of Him or not. Once you identify them, God will provide confirmation.

One common mistake is to move headlong, convinced that your dream is of God and finally realize it is not. As King Solomon said: "Many are the plans in a person's

---

5. Romans 11: 36

heart, but it is the LORD's purpose that prevails." (Proverbs 19:21). In any case, when this happens to you, you should not stop dreaming but on the contrary, you should use that disappointment to learn from your mistakes and get started again.

- **The strength of a vision**

    The clearer your vision, the more it creates in you an energy and power to bring it to pass. It helps you make appropriate decisions very early, choices regarding your studies or an activity, concentrate on things that matter, stay focused, and prevents you from wasting time and energy on all kinds of things with no purpose. It gives you a direction and a goal.

    A vision can be personal but it can be collective as well. If you realize you cannot make it alone, never hesitate to share your vision with someone else or with a group of people. There can be several possible reactions:

    - Some people embrace your vision and want to participate because it matches something that matters to them, or in some cases they have the same vision but never dared taking the plunge.

    - Some people support your vision because you are the one sharing it. They thus follow the project's initiator more than the project itself, but they trust you so much that they want to be a part of the adventure.

- Some people do not believe in your vision at all. In their opinion, it may seem far-fetched, unworkable or well beyond your skills. If you are not convinced by your project, their remarks may discourage you and even kill your vision. Nevertheless, it is always interesting to gather several opinions, as this can allow you to highlight some things you had not considered before. If you are the head of an organization, sharing your vision with your teams is highly important, for they may support your project and it is always interesting to listen to their suggestions regarding its implementation.

Many have started alone because no one believed in their vision at first, only to realize afterwards that they were right. It is the visionaries' strength. See before others, beyond the limits of what is reasonable to ordinary people.

You will be surprised to find out that the destiny of some is related to your vision. Your vision is like a puzzle and each person that adheres to it is nothing but a piece of the puzzle. The larger your vision, the more you need to surround yourself with a team. You must carefully choose the people you will work with because it is very important to always remember that it is in unified action that power will manifest.

- **Some questions to help you discover your destiny**

    - Do you know the purpose of your life? If so, what is it?

- Do you believe you have started writing "your story"?

- Do you feel you are the person you were meant to be? If not, why?

- What are the dreams rooted to the bottom of your heart that keep coming back?

- If you had the opportunity, what would you like to achieve more than anything?

3 – Passion and talents: indicative elements of destiny

- **What is passion?**

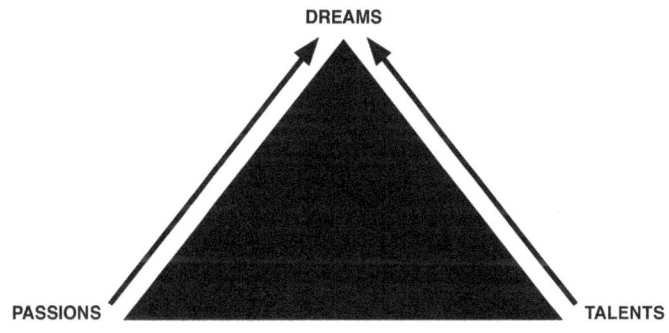

Passion is the fuel, the energy that gives you the strength to accomplish what you have been created for. It provides your mind with the motivation and determination you need to pursue your dream, by refusing the frustration of a monotonous and dull life. It acts like the gasoline giving you the energy and the will to take up challenges, overcome obstacles and episodes of discouragement, which can stand in your way.

A vision that comes from God requires so much commitment, involvement and sacrifices that it will be directly related to your passion. **When He created you, He deposited in you a passion corresponding to your call.**

One of the first steps to discover your dreams is to find out what your passions are and then search for your talents.

Even if you already know your dreams, examining your passions and talents can help you develop a better understanding of your dream and help you recognize your strengths and weaknesses involved.

- **How to identify your passions?**

Passions are directly connected to the heart and emotions. Passion is an emotion that awakens enthusiasm or excitement in you every time you practice it, talk about it or think about it. When you practice an activity connected to your passion, your heart ignites, you are like a fish in water, you lose track of time. Playing a musical instrument, doing sports, traveling, tinkering, restoring a house, solving a problem, studying a foreign language, working, teaching, helping others, are just a few examples. Your passions lead you to achieve the desires, aspirations, wishes, ambitions that are anchored in your heart, in other words, your dreams.

Here are some questions to help you identify your passions. Take some time to answer, even if the answers sometimes seem obvious. Indeed, there are things you like that seem so natural and innate that you do not even realize that they are actually passions.

- **Some questions to help you to discover your passions**

    - What do you like to do? (List your answers by order of preference)
    - What activities can you practice without paying attention to time?
    - What would be your dream job? Why?
    - What kind of books, films or television programs interest you? Why?
    - What kind of men or women inspire you? Why?
    - In general, what do you do to chase away boredom? Why?
    - If you asked your friends to describe you, what would they say you are passionate about?

4 – Frustrations

Some of your affections and frustrations can be indicators of your calling, like developers of what God has called you to. The causes of frustration can be internal or external.

An "external frustration" comes from the fact that some situations you have personally lived or witnessed affect you. We can even say that in some cases, these situations revolt you and make you face something you would like to change.

An "internal frustration" comes from a collision between the life you live and the one you aspire to live or have been called to live. In such a case, although you have a great job, good income, everything to be happy, you still feel deeply dissatisfied when you look at your life, because it is not in harmony with the script written inside you.

In 1950, during a missionary trip in India, Mother Teresa was struck when she saw the streets of Calcutta crowded with beggars, orphans and sick people. Their misery and condition affected her to the point that she decided to dedicate her life to help those ostracized by society. After being a nun, within the missionary order of the Sisters of Notre dame de Loreto (from 1929), she left the community in 1949, aged 39, to "**follow her call**" and set up her own congregation in 1950. She established several structures to welcome those who had been forgotten by the system: the unloved, the poor and the oppressed. Her beginnings as a nun had predisposed her to follow that path, but she needed that trip to India to discover her true "calling". From then on, nothing else mattered to her. Her love for others, her courage, her perseverance, her strength of character, her sensitivity, her compassion and her faith in the impossible all made her dream come true: rescue the poor, build orphanages, school street children, welcome the abandoned by society, the leprous and those suffering from AIDS. Her frustration was an indicator of what she had been called to. She passed away leaving behind her a wonderful legacy. The congregation counts some 4,500 people today, widely spread around the world, taking care of about 610 missions in 123 countries. Back then, who would have thought that this fragile-looking woman could create such an important organization, transforming millions of people's lives?

- **Some questions to help you discover your frustrations**
    - What frustrates me (internal)?
    - What affects or revolts me (external)?
    - What would I like to see change in me/ around me?
    - What do I see, which others don't see?

5 – Other channels through which God reveals destiny

In addition to the various ways mentioned above, God can also reveal your destiny in the ways that follow:

- **Through the Word of God**

By reading God's Word, you may receive the revelation of your calling. Your eyes remain fixed on a particular passage and you read it again and again until it etches itself in your mind. For some, the certainty will be immediate, while for others the confirmation will occur over a few days, even weeks, but one thing is sure: you know God has spoken to you. God always confirms His Word, He will confirm that certainty in your heart.

That is what happened to me regarding the writing of this book. I had already worked on some writing projects but had never written my own book. This desire becoming stronger and stronger in my heart, I prayed: "Father, please confirm whether you want me to write this book". A thought came to my mind, saying I should read the book of Habakkuk, chapter 2.

I opened my Bible, began reading and came across the following passage: "Then the Lord replied: "Write down the revelation and make it plain on tablets so that a herald may run with it." (Habakkuk 2:2). I then had the conviction that the time had come for me to write what God had put in my heart.

- **Through thoughts**

Thoughts are the main way used by God to communicate with His children. At the beginning of one's walk with God, it is difficult to discern the mind of God from your own thought. But as one learns to listen to God's voice, their mind becomes more and more sensitive and manages to distinguish the thought that comes from Him.

- **Through prophecy**

God can reveal your destiny through the prophetic word. That word confirms a desire you had within your heart. It strengthens your faith for it validates the aspirations you had, as truly coming from God. This confirmation gives you the assurance that you can indeed proceed, taking God's time into account.

God can also use the prophetic word to announce things He has planned for your future, but which you know nothing of. He announces them to you in advance to prepare you, so when these things happen, you may know that they indeed come from Him. Sometimes, as you listen to prophecies, you can be puzzled because it may all seem out of reach and impossible to achieve. As already seen, God does not see you as you see yourself and you should never forget that He is the one that makes you capable. As you receive this word, you are probably far from being the person you are told you will be. Maybe you are like King David who, before being anointed to be king, was a simple shepherd. God is able to do great things through your life, so when you receive such words, write them down somewhere, in order to read them later and if they truly come from God, He will confirm His word. Indeed, it is wise to always confirm that the word you have received comes from God.

Here is what the Bible says: "Dear friends, do not believe every spirit, but test the spirits to see whether they are from God, because many false prophets have gone out into the world." (1 John 4:1).

Let us look at an example of a prophetic word that has propelled a friend into her destiny:

Sophie[6] was supposed to complete her masters in law within less than two months. A few months prior, she had registered in a school of international law in Switzerland, where she wanted to do an additional year and eventually continue with her PhD. But the more the deadline was approaching, the less she was at peace with her choice. Not wanting to make a mistake, she decided to pray and get clear direction from the Lord, regarding her future. But the days kept passing and she hadn't received the confirmation nor clear direction about her future. A few days before completing her masters, she prayed the Lord and

---

6. The given name was deliberately changed.

insistently asked to be answered by the end of the week-end, because she needed to prepare for her departure to Switzerland. That week-end, at a wedding, she received a prophetic word from the person sitting next to her at the table, even though she was meeting him for the first time. He told her: "I feel you are at a crossroad and you don't know which direction to take. I see you are hesitating between two options. To go abroad or stay in Paris and you have even started getting ready to leave Paris. But I feel God wants you to stay because He has many things planned for you here and if you obey His word, He will open doors you would not expect. She was amazed and impressed by the accuracy of the prophecy. She was also touched that God heard her prayers and took time to send someone to talk to her. This word cleared up the confusion that had been haunting her heart and He replaced it with peace. She gave up her Switzerland project and decided to stay in Paris. She completed her masters as valedictorian. During the summer of that year, a large international organization contacted and offered her an internship, having found her resume on an internal database. By the end of the internship, her manager made an offer which she accepted. She was given large international projects to manage and the scale of her responsibilities never stopped increasing during the time she worked with them. The prophetic word she had received enabled her to make the right choice.

- **By discernment**

It is difficult to move on in life without purpose, without having a clear direction. Discernment allows you to distinguish between things in the physical world and in the spiritual world. It sheds light on your pathway and helps you decide which direction you should take. It helps you to be pragmatic and aim right. Always keep in mind that as the Apostle Paul said: "God has prepared things for you which the eye has not seen, ear has not yet heard, and which have not entered in your heart."[7].

Therefore, one of the keys available to the believer to dissipate confusion and clearly discern what God has planned for their life is prayer in Spirit, prayer in tongues. When the believer prays in tongues, their spirit intercedes in their stead, and the Holy Spirit uploads mysteries and revelations from heaven to their spirit, in accordance with the believer's life, as if there was a synchronization between heaven and earth. The more the believer prays in tongues, the more their spirit discerns the plans and divine projects regarding their future.

- **By the audible voice of God**

Some people have the privilege of clearly hearing the voice of God. This is primarily due to their call, which requires that they hear things directly from God. Certain promises and "predictions" can only be received and believed if they are heard directly from God.

6 – The course of destiny

"I have a dream", Martin Luther King

Martin Luther King was an African-American pastor, born in 1929 in segregated America. He came from the middle class and lived a normal youth until a particular event

---

7. 1 Corinthians 2: 9-10 (Voluntarily paraphrased).

triggered a switch in his destiny. On December 1, 1955, a black woman named Rosa Parks was arrested because she refused to give up her seat on a bus to a white passenger. The black community of Montgomery arose against the decision and decided to boycott the bus system, as a sign of protest. A movement to support Rosa Parks was formed and Martin Luther King took it over. The boycott lasted a year, during which some black people walked tens of kilometers a day to go to work. On December 21, 1956, the boycott ended after the Supreme Court of the United States of America declared segregation in public transportation, restaurants, schools and other public places, illegal.[8]

With this victory, Martin Luther King got fully involved in the struggle for equal rights in the American society. In 1963, a few steps away from the White House, in front of the Lincoln Memorial, he gave a famous symbolic speech: "I have a dream". His speech echoed throughout the world and was the beginning of profound changes in society. In 1964, the Civil Right Act declared any discrimination based on race, color of skin, religion, sex or national origin, illegal.[9] That same year, Martin Luther King received the Nobel Prize for Peace. In 1965, the Voting Right Act granted the right to vote to all American citizens, without any restriction.[10]

---

8. From the Wikipedia website: https://en.wikipedia.org/wiki/Martin_Luther_King_Jr. (consulted on January 22, 2016).
9. From the Wikipedia website: https://en.wikipedia.org/wiki/Civil_Rights_Act_of_1964 (consulted on January 22, 2016).
10. From the Wikipedia website: https://en.wikipedia.org/wiki/Martin_Luther_King_Jr. (consulted on March 13, 2016).

He was murdered in 1968 in Memphis, at 39. Despite his young age and the political future that was ahead of him, his fight was not vain, because he had accomplished with no doubt what he had been called for.

7 – Natural predispositions

When carefully looking at the life course of Joseph, Martin Luther King and Mother Teresa, it becomes obvious that they have something in common: they discovered and accomplished that for which they were born. The lives of all three have had such an impact that there still are repercussions. Yet, there was no indication from the start that their lives would take such a trajectory. And I am sure that in themselves, while they were younger, they never imagined that this was what they would later become. However, if we look back at the dreams and frustrations they faced in their time, we can notice that from their younger days, they had some predispositions that explain their background and the impact they left behind them.

- **Joseph, business management**

When we look at Joseph's life for example, we notice that when he was sold as a slave to Potiphar, he very quickly caused Potiphar's business to prosper, who in turn assigned him full responsibility of everything he owned. The Bible tells us: "When his master saw that the Lord was with him and that the Lord gave him success in everything he did, Joseph found favor in his eyes and became his attendant. Potiphar put him in charge of his household and he entrusted to his care everything he owned." (Genesis 39:

3-4). Potiphar being an officer of Pharaoh, it is assumed that besides being very prosperous, he certainly had a lot of people under him.

As seen, Joseph had access to Pharaoh thanks to his gift of dream interpretation. Yet, he never had to use that gift for Potiphar.

If Potiphar entrusted the management of all his property, it is because Joseph was able to highlight other qualities that may not have been visible at first glance, such as integrity, relationship, leadership, management, administration of goods. The years spent at Potiphar's were for Joseph a perfect preparation to discover and develop skills that would be very useful later, Joseph having to assume much higher responsibilities, later given to him by Pharaoh.

- **Mother Teresa, compassion**

Mother Teresa took Holy Orders at 19, which leaves us to assume that at that young age, her heart was already filled with compassion, mercy and love for her neighbor. Her choice to enter the missionary order of the Sisters of Our Lady of Loreto was not trivial, seeing that later she would form her own organization and spend the rest of her life in the missionary field. Her years as a missionary with the Sisters of Our Lady of Loreto were just like Joseph's case, a preparatory time which allowed her to discover and exercise her gifts, and gain the necessary experience and skills required to manage her own organization.

- **Martin Luther King, protection**

Martin Luther King had chosen to become a pastor, like his father.

The word pastor comes from the Latin word *pastor*, meaning "shepherd". In addition to shepherding the flock, shepherds also take care of it and protect it.

Those two traits - taking care and protecting - perfectly characterize Martin Luther King and led him to stand for Rosa Parks and get involved later in the struggle for equal rights. The preparation of sermons and worship taught him about the weight and the power of words and developed in him an ability and a charisma to talk and get the crowd's attention. He was an extraordinary speaker. He imposed his Christian values to refuse any form of violence, whether verbal or physical. During his studies, he discovered Henry David Thoreau and was inspired by his writings on non-violent civil disobedience, seeing how successful Gandhi was in India, with regards to fighting for the independence of his country.

When you see how Martin Luther King and his friends were repeatedly arrested and mistreated, you could believe it would have been easy for them to switch to violence. But like Jesus, they decided not to respond to violence by violence and their strategy paid off.

- **Observation**

Joseph, Mother Teresa and Martin Luther King all three showed natural predispositions that enable us to apprehend the course of their lives with a different look. All three went through three phases:

1. A preparatory phase,
2. A development phase of their character and their gifts,
3. The fulfillment of their destiny.

In view of all this, we can only admit that if their lives have been so impactful, there is certainly no coincidence: it is because they let their lives be led by the Great Conductor.

The destiny of each was clear:

- Joseph had to save the people of Israel from famine
- Mother Teresa had to bring relief and comfort to the poor and the needy
- Martin Luther King had to establish equality between black and white people

People who are sceptical about God's existence often ask the following question: "If God exists, why doesn't He interfere in such situations?"

These three stories show us that God intervened under specific circumstances, but to do so, He used His children. He made the choice to work with His sons and daughters.

When one takes this into consideration, they realize that the current situation of our society is not God's responsibility in any way, but simply the fact that there is a lot of work to do and unfortunately many workers are missing. That is the reason why God raises awareness among His children on the importance of stepping into their destiny, to participate to the construction of a better world, by responding to the needs faced by our society.

8 – The various stages of destiny

Professor Robert Clinton[11] spent more than 30 years of his life studying "Destiny": its progress, principles, requirements and effects in individuals' lives. The sum of information he gathered allowed him to establish that there is order and chronology in all stages of destiny. Let us look at them together.

- **The six steps of destiny**[12]

▶ **Step 1: Sovereign foundations**

According to the consultant Lance Wallnau, sovereign foundations[13] are all the characteristics that define one's personality. You have no control over them, because they were determined before you were born.

They correspond to:

---

11. Dr. J. Robert (Bobby) Clinton is the main Leadership professor at university: School of Intercultural Studies of Fuller Theological Seminary in Pasadena.
12. These stages are essentially inspired by the book written by Dr. R. Clinton, entitled *The Making of a Leader: recognizing the lessons and stages of leader development*, Nav Press, new edition, 2012. p.37.
13. Lance Wallnau: Believer's edge – Lesson 6: "Personal Mastery".

- Your birth year
- Your parents, your family environment
- Your country of origin and the country you grew up in
- Your character
- Your physical characteristics
- Your gifts and talents
- Your call

Your birth year, character, personality, gifts and talents, sensitivity, physical and intellectual abilities, strengths and weaknesses, passions and culture are no coincidence, or simply the genetic legacy from your parents, but they make up the identity that God wanted you to have. This may seem difficult for people who grew up in a harsh family environment, those who do not like their country of origin or even their physical appearance, but none of it is an error. It is sometimes much later that some people realize that these foundations have determined who they have become and what they have been able to accomplish.

▶ Step 2: internal development

Every child of God is called to grow constantly, both spiritually and physically. The more one grows, the more their horizon and perspective of life expand and they begin to see life from another angle: the perspective of God. Prayers, the reading of God's Word and listening to the voice of God develop and solidify the communion one has with the Maker. Your growth is done step by step, brick after brick. The process may seem long to some, but solid foundations are falling into place.

This transformation is not visible first because it primarily happens from the inside, before being visible from the outside. During that time, God tests your integrity, obedience, attitude through the trials and whether He can trust you or not. Those who respond favorably, with the right attitude, will emerge grown and fortified, ready to be entrusted greater responsibilities.

▶ Step 3: development of gifts and talents

During this period, you clearly identify what your gifts and talents are and you develop them. Their development confirms or contradicts the calling which you think is yours because, as we will see in the next chapter entitled "Discover your gifts and talents", your gifts are also indicators of your calling.

It is important to note that during stages II and III, changes occur mainly inside. Don't get discouraged if you do not accomplish anything really significant during that period, keep in mind the image of the iceberg. The submerged part is by far more significant than the visible part. It is the work that God is doing in you, He develops the inside so that the outside reflects the inside.[14]

▶ Step 4: maturity of life

At this stage of your life, you are ready to unfold and show your true nature. You now understand that the previous stages were indispensable for you to become the

---

14. Dr. Robert Clinton: *The Making of a Leader,* op. cit., p.38.

person you are today and draw closer to the heart of God. Robert Clinton even said that during this phase of your life: "your fellowship with God becomes fundamental, it is more important than your ministry's success and it is by it that you will be successful in all you will do."[15]

However, according to Lance Wallnau, 80% of people fail step 4 because they do not know or do not understand that the process they are going through aims at bringing the best out of themselves. So, they eventually end up stopping after a certain time, discouraged by trials and obstacles they encountered along the way.

▶ Step 5: Convergence

Following this maturity phase, convergence takes place between your natural gifts, spiritual gifts, passions and the different experiences you have been through. It is the most fruitful time of your life because the development of your gifts, added to your years of experience, allows you to make the most of your abilities. However, very few people reach the convergence stage because they lack personal development.

When you thoroughly look at the lives of Joseph, Mother Teresa and Martin Luther King, you find that each, in their own way, passed at least 5 stages. Their birth, the family environment they grew up in, the events or situations they faced, the decisive encounters they had, the gifts and talents they developed, etc. Each stage prepared them for the next and that is how they were able to succeed.

---

15. Dr Robert Clinton: *The Making of a Leader*, op. cit., p. 39.

▶ Step 6: Celebration

This stage corresponds to those who have been able to remain loyal and attached to God, against all odds. They are in the will of God, produce lots of fruit and bless a lot of people. They are those who have been successful in their calling and who today share their experience and wisdom. This stage is called "celebration" because those who experience it are privileged to see the fruit of their labor transform lives, cities, and for some, countries. Among these people is John Maxwell.

He was nominated "best leadership expert in the world" in May 2014, by the American magazine Inc. Magazine. He was born in 1947 in the USA. After his studies, he entered the ministry and became a pastor. In 1972, he met Curt Kampmeier, a specialist in personal development, who asked him the following question: "John, do you have a plan for your personal development?" John Maxwell answered: "No, I have no plan". At that time, he was completely clueless about personal development and its purpose. Curt Kampmeier told him: "John, growth is not an automatic thing". John Maxwell began to follow courses on personal development, because he desired to become the person God wanted him to be. After 25 years of full-time ministry, God asked him to focus on leadership and develop leaders, according to the principles of the Word of God. He obeyed and left his position at the San Diego church. Many people asked him:" John why have you abandoned the ministry?" He simply answered: "I have not left the ministry. My call is to serve people. I have done it during several years as a pastor, but today God calls me to do it differently". He wrote more than 80 books and has sold more than 19 million across the world. He also created "Equip" a non-profit organization that aims to train leaders, pastors, deacons, men and women, in leadership. "Equip" has trained 9 million people in 80 countries. He then created the John Maxwell University, together with Paul Martinelli, a school that prepares men and women to leadership. In 2013, he was invited by the President of Guatemala to talk about leadership to the most influential actors of the country (parliamentarians, high-ranking officials, CEOs, etc.). In February 2016, he was invited by the President of Paraguay to do the same. During those two events, 250 consultants of the John Maxwell University coached some 20,000 people within three days, in order to impulse change and transformation in those countries. Now being 70 years old, he keeps giving conferences around the world, in order to encourage new generations to take the lead and influence the world with the principles of the Kingdom.

John Maxwell has reached the convergence stage and now applies the celebration stage, sharing his wisdom and knowledge, so that the next generations can go higher and further than he did. His ambition is to make all the nations disciples.

9 – Obstacles to destiny

Obstacles and challenges will surely stand in your way and your faith will be more than once tested, to a point where you will even wonder at times whether you are indeed in the will of God. Overcoming all those challenges will change you and you will no longer be the same person by the end of the race, but before crossing the finishing line, you will have two enemies to destroy.

An internal one: yourself. And an external one: Satan. Contrary to popular belief, your biggest enemy is not the one outside, but rather the one inside. Your internal enemy is characterized by your fears, your doubts, your reasoning, your limits, your lack of faith, lack of rigor, discipline, perseverance, your pride. When we look at Robert Clinton's process, we see that it is precisely those character traits that God changes during the inner development phase, because your interior enemy must be defeated for you to move forward. As the African saying states: "If there's no enemy inside, the outside enemies cannot harm you".

- **Your external enemy**

As already seen, Satan is afraid that the believer fully manifests who they are in Christ. The more your calling has the ability to: change lives, give love, enlighten, give hope, solutions, lead to the truth and knowledge, preserve couples and families, build healthy foundations in society, redefine the word "success", bring God to the center of lives, help others understand the sense and purpose of life, the more you will encounter opposition. But do not get intimidated nor even discouraged. Keep your eyes fixed on the One who will give you the strength to be more than a conqueror.

- **Your internal enemy**

  ▶ **The lack of knowledge**

One of the biggest enemies of the believer is the lack of knowledge. This is not me saying it, but God Himself: "my people perish for a lack of knowledge" (Hosea 4:6).

How many wasted lives and aborted fate because of the lack of knowledge? Knowledge enables you to know who God is and who you are in Him. It allows you to be rooted in the truth, to have a firm, unwavering faith and prevents you from being like a storm-tossed boat, relying on wind, circumstances and news but, on the contrary, it helps you make sound choices and right decisions, because your confidence is based on the promises in the Word of God.

Solutions:

King Salomon said: "For wisdom will enter your heart, and knowledge will be pleasant to your soul." (Proverbs 2:10). Let us look at some keys to develop one's knowledge of God:

- **Delight in reading the Word** to discover the meaning of life, not according to the criteria of society but according to God. Regular reading waters your mind and feeds it with spiritual food and the knowledge it needs to make the right choices and decisions.

- **Develop an intimacy with the Holy Spirit** to receive the revelations for your life.

- **The knowledge of the Word** and revelations communicated by the Holy Spirit will strengthen your faith.

▶ **Fear**

Some of the dreams that God gave you seem scary, and you feel small in front of them. They involve taking risks and making sacrifices that you are not always willing to make. For some, it may be to change jobs, go back to school, take a training, or it may be to invest all your savings, ask the bank for a loan, find partners, start from scratch, etc.

Your life is pleasant and you do not wish to put at risk the balance, sense of security and comfort that you have built over time. Yet, you know that God is with you, but the fear of failure paralyzes you and you prefer to postpone your project.

Solutions:

- **Rely on God** and not on your own strengths. The Apostle Paul wrote: "For the Spirit God gave us does not make us timid, but gives us power, love and self-discipline." (2 Timothy 1:7).

- **Have the courage to reject the status quo** and step out of your comfort zone.

- **Surround yourself with good people** who will be able to help you with their advice, their personal experiences and their maturity

- **Move forward step by step**. Often, your dream is too big for you. Therefore, divide it into several small steps to advance gradually.

- **Do not be afraid of failure**. As the inventor Thomas Edison said: "I don't get discouraged because any unsuccessful attempt we leave behind is another step forward."

▶ The lack of faith

"Now faith is confidence in what we hope for and assurance about what we do not see." (Hebrews 11:1). Faith is the foundation of the Christian life. It is faith that pushes you towards action and allows you to believe that nothing is impossible to God. The lack of faith, however, paralyzes you and forces you to continue to evolve in environments you master. It prevents you from laying hold of God's promises for your life, from bringing God's realities to earth in order to fully manifest the nature of Jesus that resides in you.

Solution:

- **Reading** the Bible, listening to the sermons and testimonials activates and strengthens your faith. When your friends or your reasoning say that it is not possible, rely on the Word of God and the promises He gave you. As the Word says:" Consequently, faith comes from hearing the message, and the message is heard through the word about Christ." (Romans 10:17).

▶ Reasoning, thoughts

Reasoning is one of the worst enemies of faith, because it tries to make rational what is irrational. In other words, it attempts to bring the realities of the spiritual realm to your level of understanding. It is good to reason, to analyze what you are told, not to believe anything, but it is a fact that faith and reasoning are opposed. Faith is "the conviction about the unseen", while reasoning relies on evidence and tangible things.

Solution:

- **Do not be overwhelmed by fear,** but rather put your confidence in God. He will ask you to do things that will be beyond your comprehension because He wants you to learn to walk not with your natural eyes, but with your spiritual eyes, the eyes of faith. Pastor Myles Munroe one day said on this subject: "The worst enemy of the vision is the view".

▶ **The lack of obedience and of sanctification**

When God calls His children to follow His recommendations and walk in sanctification, it is to protect them from making mistakes that could have fatal consequences on their lives. Many people close the doors of blessings on themselves and fail in their Christian walk, by lack of obedience and sanctification. The Bible says:

> For the flesh desires what is contrary to the Spirit, and the Spirit what is contrary to the flesh. They are in conflict with each other, so that you are not to do whatever you want. (Galatians 5:17)

Solutions:

- **Understand obedience to God** because it is for your own good, to protect you, so that you walk in peace and blessing. God's instructions, even if they can seem difficult at times, are good and perfect for you because they were given to protect you. God takes pleasure in obedience, because in His eyes obedience is better than sacrifices.[16]

- One of the solutions, in order to walk in obedience and sanctification, is **to develop your spirit to dominate over your flesh and its contrary desires.**

- **Develop your spirit, your mind,** because some fights are hard to carry out alone and the assistance of the Holy Spirit is necessary in order to walk, not according to the flesh but according to the Spirit.

- **Surround yourself with people** who encourage you.

▶ **The lack of rigor, discipline**

Rigor and discipline are the two essential elements to continually grow, and especially to make it to the end. Without them, you will tend to relax after a while and seek ease. It is true that today, it is easy to get distracted and waste time with all sorts of activities. Experience has shown me that it is not always the brightest that succeeds, but those who know how to be rigorous and disciplined. The Word of God uses, on several occasions, words of encouragement to keep the People of God moving forward without giving up, such as: "Be strong and take courage" (Joshua: 1:6).

---

16. 1 Samuel 15: 22.

Solution:

*"**Discipline** is the bridge between goals and accomplishments",* Jim Rohn. Discipline allows you to keep an eye on your goals, to persevere, to stay on course in the face of adversity and discouragement. It gives you the strength to work while your friends are having fun, to take classes on week-ends and evenings, to work overtime, to save when you are tempted to spend, to learn a new job, to reduce the time you spend watching television, etc. Applied daily, discipline will help you adopt reflexes that will enable you to better use your spare time, to better organize your priorities throughout the day, to take time every day or every week and dedicate it to the building of your dream.

Chapter 4
Your gifts and talents

1 – Your destiny within you

Perhaps you are not always aware of it, but your greatest wealth lies in you: your gifts and talents. It is important to know them because they are the tools that will help you build your destiny. The more you exercise them, the more you will develop your skills and increase your potential. The realization of your dreams is therefore dependent on the good use you make of them, as well as the experience you gain from exercising them. The Bible tells us that one day, God said to Moses that He wanted the people to build Him a tabernacle, so that He would dwell among them. This sacred place would be the location where the Ark of the Covenant would dwell. The Ark of the Covenant symbolized at that time the presence of God. He therefore gave detailed instructions to Moses concerning the Ark, such as the surface area of the tabernacle, the materials to be used, the elements and symbols that should be inside and outside.

The construction of the whole required ingenuity, intelligence, skills and technical knowledge that no one had. God explained to Moses that He had chosen men among the people, to whom He had given the intelligence and the skills to create this piece of work.

The Bible says:

> Then the Lord said to Moses, "See, I have chosen Bezalel son of Uri, the son of Hur, of the tribe of Judah, and I have filled him with the Spirit of God, with wisdom, with understanding, with knowledge and with all kinds of skills - to make artistic designs for work in gold, silver and bronze, to cut and set stones, to work in wood, and to engage in all kinds of crafts. Moreover, I have appointed Oholiab son of Ahisamak, of the tribe of Dan, to help him. Also I have given ability to all the skilled workers to make everything I have commanded you (...)". (Exodus 31: 1-6)

In other passages of the Bible, we see that God equips men for the mission He entrusts them with. This passage is very interesting, because it illustrates the fact that it is God who makes each individual capable, by entrusting them with gifts and talents, according to their mandate.

- **What is the call?**

Often, the ailments and frustrations you suffer from are indicators of what God calls you to. God cannot ask you to do something if He has not given you the preliminary capacity to accomplish it. When God asks you to do something, it means that He has already given you the ability, even if it still seems beyond your skills. But as you obey and trust Him, you see new abilities and skills you had never been aware of before, emerge in you.

Talents are, like ailments, frustrations and passions, clues that point towards the direction of your calling. It is therefore important to discover them.

- **What is talent?**

A gift is a provision, a natural and innate quality, while **a talent** is an ability, a capacity given by God, according to your destiny. Each person is born with one or several talents that will be used on one or several occasions during their lifetime. Talent is the indicator of a person's potential because it allows them to accomplish things with greater ease, control and success than others.

2 – Discovering one's talents

The discovery of your talents can happen in several ways.

- **Talents you are aware of**

There are talents which you are aware of: those you have clearly identified, because you found out on your own that you were more gifted than others in some areas, or that you had more ease, or simply because the people who know you well highlighted them. Once you identify those talents, you need to exercise and develop them to their maximum potential. Unfortunately, many people do not take care of their talents, because they see no value in them and are not aware that these are the instruments that God has placed within them to fulfill their destiny.

- **The talents you are not aware of**

There are talents which you are not yet aware of, until a particular situation makes you so. You then decide to start little by little, with practice. You realize that you love what you do and you are even gifted so much that people around you point it out. There are people who think they have no talent at all, because they grew up in an environment in which one constantly belittled them through criticism or demeaning words. They eventually internalize the negative remarks such as: "you have no talent", "you are incapable", "you suck" ... Others have lost confidence in themselves because of their failures and setbacks in life. They are convinced that they have no talent.

In both cases, the concerned people often evolve in environments where they are bad at what they do or averagely succeed, while being frustrated. If you feel your talent is not very efficient in the field in which you evolve, it is better to seek for an environment within which you are truly gifted, so that you truly flourish in practicing your talent.

Finally, there are those who do things with such ease that they don't even realize that they are gifted, because it seems normal to them. There are many other cases but these few examples may reassure those who believe they have no talent. Every one of us has at least one, as we will see in the next chapter on talent management.

- **The gifts and talents that God reveals**

   There are also the gifts and talents that God reveals. Let us suppose you have just discovered your destiny and realized that God called you to accomplish things that are completely different from the ones you had usually been doing. Panic strikes because you feel totally incapable.

   As previously seen, God can give you projects that are difficult because He wants to stimulate your faith, teaching you to no longer rely on your own strength but rather to lean on Him, to have trust in Him. When you decide to obey by faith, God then activates the gifts He has placed in you. That is exactly what happened to the writer and pastor John Bevere.

   In 1991, he received a clear word from the Lord in his heart, saying: "my son, I want you to write". He rejected this idea, believing that his writing skills were too poor when he was a student to consider writing anything. Ten months later, two women came to see him two weeks apart and delivered the same message: "John if you do not write the books God has given you to write, He will give them to someone else. But you will be judged for not having done it"[1]. Seized with fear, he obeyed and started to write. He

---

1. John Bevere: *Draw close to Him*, Ed. Vida, p.5

was surprised to notice that as he was writing, he received ideas and thoughts that were not coming from him, but that were inspired by the Holy Spirit. To this day, he has written more than a dozen books, many of which are best-sellers.

- **A few tips to help you discover your talents:**

  - Ask your loved ones what gifts and talents they see in you.

  - Take time to think about things that are difficult for others but relatively easy to you.

  - Try new activities you care about: this is a great way to perhaps discover talents that you completely ignore.

- **Some questions to help you discover your talents:**

  - Have you already identified some of your gifts and talents? If so, which ones?

  - Ask five people what talents they see in you. Compare their responses with the list you made previously.

  - In which areas do your friends always request your help?

  - What activities give you real satisfaction?

  - In what areas do you understand and do things more easily than others?

3 – Talent management

- **The parable of the talents**

Jesus liked to use parables and images when teaching His disciples about the mysteries of creation and the Kingdom of God. One day, He told them the parable of the talents.[2]

This parable tells us about three servants who had received one or more talents[3] from their master, before he left for a trip. They were ordered to increase them. The first received five talents, the second two talents and the third, one talent. After some time, the master came back from his travels and asked each of them to report on how they had managed the talents during his absence. The first and the second had grown their talents, but not the third. The master's verdict regarding the third servant was irrevocable: "And the useless servant, throw him in the outer darkness, where there will be weeping and gnashing of teeth." (Matthew 25: 30).

The term used by the master to qualify the third servant is very important, because he says he is "useless". The dictionary gives the following definition of the word useless: "That cannot be used, that is basket case, bootless, disadvantageous, fruitless, futile, hopeless, idle, impractical,

---

2. Parable of the talents: Matthew 25: 14-30.
3. The word "talent" corresponds in this parable to a monetary unit which was used in ancient Greece. At that time one talent's weight is equivalent to 60 mines (6 mines is equivalent to 25.86kg of silver), from the website of Wikipedia: https://en.wikipedia.org/wiki/Talent_(measurement) (consulted on September 13, 2015).

ineffective, ineffectual, of no use, pointless, profitless, unavailing, unproductive, unworkable, vain, valueless, worthless".

The primary vocation of the servant was to serve his master: this was the purpose of his function. Seeing he hadn't fulfilled his task, the master considered that he was useless and ordered to get rid him.

The fact that he hadn't practiced the talent given to him somehow was disobedience and therefore, led him to being sentenced. It is true that it seems cruel, as he had not lost the talent that was given to him. But there is a powerful lesson this story teaches us about our lives. This story shows us that any element, not used in accordance with the function attributed by its creator, will be considered useless.

It is so in the Kingdom of God. When we look at other teachings of Jesus to His disciples, we see that He repeatedly emphasizes the importance of bearing fruit. In other words, to do the works that attest of His goodness, His mercy but also His creativity, His wisdom, His intelligence (Ephesians 2:10).

Like the servants of the parable, it is our responsibility to draw closer to the one who gives, so that He shares with us the nature of the mission, as well as the means at our disposal to be successful.

- **The vine and the branches**[4]

One day, Jesus used the image of the vine and the branches to instruct the disciples on the importance of bearing fruit. He said to them:

---

4. John 15: 1-8

> I am the true vine, and my Father is the gardener. **He cuts off every branch in me that bears no fruit,** while every branch that does bear fruit He prunes so that it will be even more fruitful. (John 15:1)

If you paraphrase the words of Jesus, you can say: "anyone who follows me but does not fulfill the purpose for which they are on earth, is of no use and therefore my Father removes that person from the Kingdom of God. On the other hand, those who bear fruit, my Father prunes them, that is to say they may be perfected and bear more fruit, because this is how the Father will be glorified".

- **Lessons to learn from these two illustrations**

The parable of the talents and the parable of the vine and the branch both have a common point, in clearly showing us God's point of view regarding the elements of creation that do not function as they have been assigned. Although these teachings are presented in the form of stories and parables, one should not neglect their message: **all things exist for a purpose.**

The Sun produces light and heat, clouds produce the rain that waters the Earth, the Earth produces the fruits, and these fruits feed man, etc. If tomorrow one of these elements was to no longer fulfill its role, the consequences on the cycle of life would be catastrophic. From this principle, one now understands better that if our society is confronted with so many problems, it is also because many people do not play the part they should in the "cycle of life" in society, simply because they do not fulfill the role

God attributed to them. Even though they work, participate to community life, vote, pay taxes, their contribution is not as it should have normally been, had they entered their destiny. We will see this in the following chapter.

4 – The development of gifts and talents

As said previously, growth is not automatic: it must be intentional. The lack of growth may even at a given time prevent you from fulfilling your calling (as per Robert Clinton's 6 stages). The author John Maxwell calls this the "law of the lid". He noticed that growth, even the sustainability of an organization, a department or a career, depends on the ability a person has to continue growing. The more a person takes time to grow, spiritually, intellectually, personally, and so on, the more that person's potential and capacity to accomplish what they were born for, grows. Looking at the lives of men and women who have been successful in their ministry, in entrepreneurship, sports, music, education, innovation, research, etc., it is obvious that such people have never interrupted the progress inside them. You can be the most talented person in the world, if you do not take time to develop the talent God has given you, you will stagnate at some point. On the other hand, the more you grow, the more your actions will be marked by qualities and influential people around you.

♦ The story of King David

When thinking of King David's life, most of us immediately think of his epic battle against the giant Goliath and his courage when he killed the one who was terrorizing a whole army. The story of this young man is very special because it shows us how a man chosen by God, a simple shepherd, became the king of a nation and made this people one of the most powerful and successful in that time and this, within a 40-year period of time.

His life story has similarities with Joseph's in many ways, as God was with him from the beginning. But what we tend to forget is that he rose to the highest office in the nation, because he never ceased growing in character, skills and intimacy with God, throughout his life.

- **Development of King David's gifts and talents.**

    Let us look at how a simple shepherd became a king.

    - **David's talent for the fight**
        - Around 17, David was anointed king by the Prophet Samuel.
        - Shortly after that, he fought the giant Goliath and won for the people of Israel.
        - Thanks to his victory against Goliath, Saul placed David at the head of his army. David went on and succeeded everywhere Saul sent him. He pleased everyone, including Saul's servant. The Bible says that he succeeded in all he undertook and that the Lord was with him (1 Samuel 18:14).

    - **David's talent for music**
        - Like for Joseph, God created an opportunity to bring David closer to King Saul. Saul was tormented by an evil spirit sent by the Lord

because of his disobedience and whenever David played the harp, Saul was relieved. Thus, David accessed the royal court.

- **David's talent to be king**

- War lord, personality of a hero, popularity among people.

- Jealous of David's reputation, Saul tried on several occasions to kill him. David had to escape from the king's court and lived as a fugitive. But some of his men followed and remained loyal to him. During that period of time, he could have killed Saul on many occasions, but he never did because of the respect he had for Saul and his position as king.

- Man of honor and value

- Loyalty of his men towards him

- Saul eventually died, but his personal guard and his family continued to be at war against David. The Bible says: "David **became increasingly stronger**, and the house of Saul was weakening" (2 Samuel 3:1).

The Hebrew word used for strong is *chazeq*, which means "stronger, higher". We can thereby understand that David was going higher and higher, from progress to progress, achievement to achievement.

At the age of 30, 13 years after being anointed by the Prophet Samuel, he became king. During all those years, David kept going higher and higher, which made him ready to be the king. David was not king just because God had decided so, but rather because during those 13 years he had developed the charisma of a leader, as well as the qualities and skills that made him legitimate in the eyes of God and the people. These years of preparation allowed him to develop:

- His intimacy with God
- His qualities as war lord and leader in time of war
- Charisma
- His qualities as spiritual leader, leader of men and leader of a nation

When looking at the course of his life, we clearly find the 6 steps mentioned by Robert Clinton: the sovereign foundations, inner development, development of talents, maturity of life, convergence and celebration. In fact, each of these steps allowed him to move to a higher level. After acceding to the throne, he put the people of Israel back on track. It became the most prosperous nation in the whole world. He put an end to the wars against the surrounding peoples. He wrote the book of Psalm, one of the most beautiful books of the Bible. He was able to do what he was created for, because he never ceased to grow throughout his whole life.

The life of King David reminds us that the believer's life should not be limited to "things to do", but rather "things to become". It is when you become the person you were meant to be that you can accomplish what you have been called to and that God is made manifest through your life. Often, when men limit themselves to their accomplishments, God sees further: He looks from the heart. A heart that reveals His nature..

Chapter 5
Destined to change the world

One day, a friend was speaking of his fiancée and with sparkling eyes, he told me: "when I was single, I never felt the need to have someone in my life, because I was alright alone. But from the time I met this girl, I often wonder how I coped without her before". Before knowing her, he didn't need to have someone in his life. After meeting and getting to know her, he realized he could no longer live without her, because she had enlightened things in his heart which only she could fill.

This is the case between Man and God. Man is satisfied with his life until the day he becomes aware that something much better exists, something that will give him more satisfaction than anything he has known before. A large number of testimonies, from atheists or people who were not interested in God, highlight the radical change in their lives when they made that encounter, the one that would impact their existence for ever, the day when they *saw* God. In other words, it is because they *saw* Him that they *believed*.[1]

The Bible tells us that the only way to "see" God is not through a pair of magical glasses but through Jesus Christ.

Indeed, Jesus came to reveal the Father. The message He brought, His teachings, wisdom, love and the works He did, all made the Father *visible* to the crowd that followed Him and to those who witnessed the healings and miracles He performed. He Himself said: "He who has seen me has seen the Father." (John 14:9). The sons and daughters of God are now responsible to make God visible to the eyes of men and through Jesus. The destiny of an entire generation depends on the destiny of the people of God. This is why the Bible says that: "For the creation waits with **eager longing** for the revelation of the sons of God". When the sons of God are revealed, they make God visible, real and authentic to those who do not know Him.

1 – Change thanks to a new reform[2]

For several centuries, Christianity has been suffering from a deterioration of its image. Its ethics and principles are today considered as obsolete, while the general feeling is that of a cold and austere representation. According to

---

1. This affirmation automatically leads to a question for non-believers: Can one see God? The answer is yes, with the eyes of faith. Doesn't the Bible say that: "Faith is the reality of what we hope for, the proof of what we don't see?" Faith gives you such a firm conviction, that what is not visible to the eyes of men is seen by spiritual eyes.
2. The use of the word reform here is in reference to the reform of Martin Luther King, the father of Protestantism.

this type of reasoning, all this is dedicated to those who need to believe in something, to feeble-minded people. It is many people's tune until a relative or life circumstances lead them to ask themselves questions that will take them closer to God. They then realize that it is not a religion, but rather a strong love relationship which unites God to His sons and daughters. This relationship they now have with Him changes the idea they had of the Christian life and of life itself. The writer John Bevere was one of these people, whose perception changed when he discovered who God was.

In his book entitled "Extraordinary is the life that is destined to you", he writes:

> I saw Christianity as void of life. Becoming a Christian meant giving up on creativity, excellence, passion, the opportunity to succeed in business, sports, in politics and other areas of life. I then didn't know but my point of view was the opposite of the life that God had destined for us because He Himself had instilled in us the desire for the extraordinary. (...) We were created to reflect the nature of God. A remarkable, amazing, extraordinary life which is not reserved exclusively to some people or some jobs, no matter who you are or what you do in life. You were created for extraordinary achievements there where God

placed you. The power to perform remarkable things and to live a life of exception is not related to an occupation but to the disposition of the heart.[3]

Many would be surprised to discover that life with God has so much more to offer than life without Him. But they ignore it because of ideological, dogmatic and philosophical walls that have been built for centuries between God and men. These barriers have estranged them from God's thought and His heart. Blaise Pascal said: "God is hidden but He lets Himself be found by those who seek Him."[4] The issue is that today, very few actually seek Him, because the idea they have of God is based on religious stories and often marked by intellectual trends that deny His existence, or deist thoughts that allow to steer a middle course.

God can attract men and women in a thousand and one ways but He mainly does it through His children. The children of God are the bridge between Him and the non-believers, because they present God as He really is (His divinity, His heart, His power). This is how the desire to know Him will emerge in people's heart and as they seek Him, He will reveal Himself to them.

The new generation yearns for a deep change. It is tired of wars, terrorist attacks, racial tensions, inequality… The time has come for the people of God to stand up and restore hope by bringing concrete solutions to the challenges that the people face, whether they are physical, emotional, spiritual, or also financial and political. But for this to happen, the life of the Spirit must regain first position in people's

---

3. John Bevere: *Extraordinaire, la vie qui vous est destinée*, Ed. Vida, 2010, p.319
4. Jean Mesnard and Blaise Pascal: *Textes inédits, p. 33*

lives, the place of honor. Only the Holy Spirit is able to solve problems and convey life, peace and hope. It is only this way that God will become a reality for our fellow citizens, being at the heart of their situation. But this will not happen without a reform of mentalities, a reform of the Church and Christianity. Several signs are showing us that this will take place, not in any political way, but through a generation of men and women filled with the Holy Spirit.

- **Jesus' "political agenda" and the reform of the Church**

In our contemporary societies, in order to implement a reform, a political program has to be defined first. Remember when Jesus began His ministry: He read an *inauguration* speech to the people. We would today call it a political program. Here is what He said:

> The Spirit of the Lord is on me, because he has anointed me to proclaim **good news** to the poor. He has sent me to **proclaim freedom for the prisoners and recovery of sight for the blind, to set the oppressed free, to proclaim the year of the Lord's favor**. (Luke 4:18-19)

The speech of Jesus clearly announces what He came for: to free creation. There are six very important points which are still up-to-date nowadays:

- Announce good news

- Heal those who have a broken heart (emotional healing)

- Deliver the captives

- Heal the blind (physical and spiritual healing)

- Let the oppressed go free

- Publish a year of grace

Let us briefly look at each of these points, in order to apply them when our turn comes and see God become a reality for everyone around us.

- **Announce good news**

The word Gospel comes from a Greek word which means "good news". The four gospels, according to Matthew, Mark, Luke, and John, announce the good news of salvation and the Kingdom of God.

There are countless people who met God without anyone mentioning Him, just by simply reading the Bible.

Philippe, one of my friends, started asking questions and showing interest in God. However, he wanted God to reveal Himself personally to him, to prove His existence. So, he prayed the following prayer: "If God exists, I want Him to talk to me. Otherwise, I will continue to live my life without Him". Shortly after this prayer, as he was withdrawing money from the ATM, a couple of elderly people approached and said: "Sir, can we bother you for a second?". A bit suspicious, Philippe responded: "Yes". The couple said: "Well, we simply wanted to offer you the Gospel of John and wish that you read chapter 3 and verse 7". Philippe went back home and full of curiosity, he opened the Gospel and began to read: "Jesus answered: 'Very truly I tell you, no one can enter the kingdom of God unless they are born of water and the Spirit. Flesh gives birth to flesh, but the Spirit gives birth to spirit.'" As he read those words, he realized that not only had God used two strangers to meet him, but the word he had just read was addressed to him directly, inspired by the Holy Spirit.

- **Heal those who have a broken heart (emotional healing)**

How many people today suffer from a lack of love or emotional wounds, caused by a painful past, abandonment, contempt, lack of recognition, loneliness, etc.? The Bible says: "You shall love your neighbor as yourself" (Mark 12:31).

This verse may seem utopian today, but if everyone applied it, be certain that most families, professionals, past and present geopolitical conflicts could have never existed. This would allow for family reconciliations, end of disputes, attacks and thefts, closure of jails and courts.

Man was designed to love and be loved, it is his nature. The Apostle Paul tells of the virtues of true love. He says:

> Love is patient, love is kind.
> It does not envy, it does not
> boast, it is not proud. It does
> not dishonor others, it is not

> self-seeking, it is not easily angered, it keeps no record of wrongs. Love does not delight in evil but rejoices with the truth. It always protects, always trusts, always hopes, always perseveres. Love never fails. (1 Corinthians 13: 4-8)

Love has such power that no heart, even the hardest, can resist it. It is impossible to count the number of men and women who can testify that their life changed the day they met love. God is love. The love that is in Man is therefore a feature of the very nature of God.

The children of God have received the love of God in their heart, as the verse tells us: "The love of God is widespread in our heart by the Holy Spirit who has been given." (Romans 5:5). The sons and daughters of God who manifest the love of God make the character of God visible. This love breaks the ice, transforms the hearts of stone into hearts of flesh (Ezekiel 11:19), establishes peace and heals the deepest wounds. How many people need to experience such love today?

- **Deliver the captives**

In the previous chapters, we saw that some people are victims of generational curses, demonic possessions or addictions that destroy them and their relationships. The sons and daughters of God have received the power to drive away demons, "to walk on snakes and scorpions and on all powers of the enemy, and nothing can harm them" (Luke 10:19).

Like Moses, the people of God are called to release those who are prisoners of the enemy. He can do it with the authority of the name of Jesus and the power of the Holy Spirit. Let us look together at a testimony that illustrates the authority the children of God have over the spiritual world:

One day, a nurse and Christian friend had a schizophrenic patient. The patient said she heard a voice asking her to mutilate and hurt herself and whenever the nurse would enter the room, the voice stopped. This patient was unaware that she was possessed, but the demon had recognized that the nurse was a child of God. This allowed the nurse to better understand the cause of her troubles and disorders.

- **Healings**

The Acts of the Apostles recounts the beginnings of the Church and Christianity. The main actor is the Holy Spirit. Throughout the entire book, we see Him leading the disciples and using them to teach and heal those they meet along their way. The disciples and first apostles' ministry was really characterized by powerful healings, leaving no doubt that God was with them.

The Bible says: "For the Kingdom of God is not in words, but in power." (1 Corinthians 4: 20). The word power is here referring to the person of the Holy Spirit. In other words, the Kingdom of God is not only the Word of God, but it is also a demonstration of the power of God.

Today, healings, signs and miracles are unfortunately not as numerous as in the days of the Acts of the Apostles, but a revival is announced. A generation of men and women is rising, with the desire to finally live the realities of the Kingdom of God. A generation that is frustrated by the gap between what is written in the Bible and the reality of what they live, on a daily basis. This generation wants to make God visible to the eyes of men. The frustration is sometimes necessary to get out of the *status quo*. This frustration pushes one to seek God, to discover the person of the Holy Spirit and to develop an intimacy with Him, in order to experiment supernatural things on earth. However, one should not seek the Holy Spirit just for the miracles, but rather for who He is and then, the miraculous will occur in their life.

A young Christian girl once told me that one day, with friends, she met a man who was suffering from a knee problem and who was hardly walking. They started talking to him about Jesus and after a while, they offered to pray for him. The man accepted, they prayed, and he was healed instantly, right on the street! This situation reminds us of the Acts of the Apostles, where the shadow of a disciple of Christ could heal a sick person (Acts 5:15). The return to that book is in motion.

- **Let the oppressed go free**

Jesus said: "So if the Son sets you free, you will be free indeed." (John 8:36). In our Western societies, slavery still exists. It is no longer agricultural or domestic but internal to the soul. Its masters are called anguish, anxiety, fear, alcoholism, etc. Although they are physically free, people are chained by their thoughts.

One of my friends was addicted to nicotine, cannabis and alcohol. After meeting God, he kept fighting these addictions. One day, at a Christian rally, the pastor asked the ones who needed prayer to move to the front. My friend walked closer and cried for God to be freed. The power of the Holy Spirit fell on him and he was instantly delivered, while he had been suffering from these addictions for a decade. The sons and daughters of God have been freed and the freedom they received allows them to inform those who are still chained that freedom is also possible.

- **Publish a year of grace**

The original Greek word used in this passage for grace is *dektos*, which means "favorable". Jesus came to bring favor, God's life blessings, to the one who follows Him. Someone who has the *special favor* of God succeeds in everything they do, attracts triumph and divine connections, opens closed doors and overcomes adversity. This grace draws people to you and leads them to God. The revelation of the sons and daughters of God is to manifest Christ, in character and in works. We just saw some of these works. If each child of God, individually, in their environment, works to announce the good news, prays for the sick and restores the broken hearted, we will definitely see hearts changed and lives transformed. But the program is not limited to that, because each child of God has been equipped to accomplish a particular work.

- **"The Metron"**

The Apostle Paul says: "but to each one of us grace has been given according to the measure [metron] of the gift of Christ." (Ephesians 4:7). In this passage from Paul, the Greek word used for measurement is *metron*, which means "a measure", but also "a limited portion". That word allows us to understand that God assigns a portion of grace to each of His children, to help them accomplish what they were created for, in addition to the gifts that help them achieve what He expects from them. This portion of grace is visible in your life when you operate in your sphere and that is what will influence the people around you, because they will soon notice that there is a special favor in your life. It is therefore very important to be where you should be, because as nature teaches us so well, it is difficult for a tree to bear fruit when in the wrong place.

I will share the experience of a couple of friends to illustrate my point. In January 2016, Kanda and Maïté left France to move to Kinshasa, Congo, to open orphanages, as well as educational and sports structures. They left everything behind them: their jobs, families and friends to answer the call of God they had received a few years earlier. Once there, they needed a vehicle to move around. They contacted one of their friends, who had graciously lent them a 4WD the previous year. They asked to rent the same vehicle or possibly buy it. Unfortunately, in the meantime, the vehicle had been sold. But their friend suggested that they should meet and discuss. They met at a restaurant and during the conversation, he asked the driver to park the vehicle in front of the glass door where they were eating and told them: "I have another solution to help you. I'm giving you my 4WD, that is my contribution to your foundation. Is that ok with you?" His 4WD was brand new, worth about 30,000 euros. This story shows us that God's favor touches hearts, opens doors and creates divine connections promoting the fulfillment of your destiny. This favor accompanied this couple who chose to obey the call of God and move where He asked them to.

2 – Change through the seven spheres of influence

A *sphere of influence* is a specific area which, through its reach, has the ability to influence the thinking systems, the cultures of millions, even billions of people around the world. The globalization of information, the development of satellite television, the Internet and social networks, now offer a much wider dissemination of geopolitical, social or cultural events that take place around the world.

The major groups, whether they are political, sports, musical or other, use these means to reach their targets (customers, fans, supporters, etc.) and incite them to join. For example, a consumer

who needs to buy a product, finding themselves in front of a multitude of options, no longer has a choice only based on quality-price ratio but also on the brand and service. Major groups no longer simply sell products but also their brand culture. In 1975, Bill Bright, the founder of campus Crusade For Christ[5] and Loren Cunningham, the founder of Youth with a Mission[6], each received a list of seven spheres of influence inspired by God that could transform a

---

5. Campus Crusade For Christ is a Christian missionary organization founded in 1951 by Bill Bright, which objective is to evangelize and train disciples in more than 190 countries around the world.
6. Youth with a Mission is an interconfessional missionary organization, implanted in 149 countries.

nation. They did not know that each had received the same list, before meeting and speaking about it. The list went as follows:

- **Religion**
- **Family**
- **Education**
- **Government (law)**
- **Media**
- **Arts & leisure**
- **Economy (business, finance, new technologies)**

Let us carefully look at this list of seven spheres and see in which way the people of God can use them to reveal the culture of the Kingdom of God to their relatives, friends, relationships, etc. The author John Maxwell, in his book entitled "The 21 irrefutable laws of leadership"[7], speaks of **the law of image.**

According to him, this law resides in the fact that a person repeats someone's actions, if considering it good for them. He explains that it is easier for a person to memorize and repeat what they see than what they simply hear. In the same way, children learn from their parents and build their identities by reproducing what they have seen them do. This can also be compared to the principle of influence:

---

7. John Maxwell, *The 21 Irrefutable Laws of Leadership*, Ed. Thomas Nelson (reedition: September 2007).

a person is naturally influenced by someone they esteem or by something that produces a positive effect on them (or negative in some cases).

a) Religion

Religion is a sphere whose influence varies according to the country (political models) and cultures. In North African countries for example, the Muslim religion is an integral part of the culture and impacts the inhabitants' lives. In Europe, although Christianity has in the past helped build the cultural identity of many nations, the number of Christians has considerably declined. When looking at a world map, it is interesting to notice that some geographical areas are dominated by this or that religion. Indeed, years ago, when a country was influential, the neighboring countries tended to adopt its religion, culture, language and rites. God has chosen a people through which He could reveal Himself to the world: the people of Israel. From this people came the Bible, the prophets, the Messiah, the disciples and the first apostles. God's objective was to see Israel radiate in the Middle Eastern region through its economy, wealth, laws, justice and wisdom, so that other nations could be intrigued by its success. Thus, by showing interest in it, they would end up turning to the source of that success: God Himself. Today, the people of God is composed of men and women, young and old, of all skin color, from every nation, whose mission is to shine within their respective communities.

b) The family

"Honor your father and your mother, as the Lord your God has commanded you, so that you may live long and that it may go well with you in the land the LORD your God is giving you." (Deuteronomy 5:16). The family is the privileged place, the place where the child builds their character, personality and identity. It is the pillar of society because it promotes growth, education, development and the process of evolving from childhood to adulthood. The wealth of a country resides in its children and their ability to apprehend life and the future. They first inherit this vision from their parents, then from society and everything related to education, values, standards, prospects, etc. it can convey.

The traditional family structure has changed in recent decades with the increasing number of divorces, splits, single-parent and blended families, and same-sex marriages. In the first chapter, we saw that depression was the primary cause of disease for young people aged 10 to 19 and suicide the third cause of death. In order to see whether there is a cause-and-effect relationship between the destructuring of the family and depression among the youth, let us look together at some figures suggested by an American study on single-parent families. This study concerns children who grew up without a father figure at home. It notes that:

- 90% of runaways grew up without a father
- 80% of children in psychiatric hospital grew up without a father
- 70% of children in correctional center grew up without a father

- 85% of adolescents in prison grew up without a father

- 70% of pregnant teenage girls grew up without a father

These figures corroborate the fact that the roles of father and mother are paramount for the balance of the child, because they each bring a model to which children can refer. However, in order to have children in good emotional health, the parents themselves must be in good emotional health. The role of the people of God is therefore to have marriages and families that are doing well, in order to help and give advice to families who are going through difficult times.

c) Education

Education is the second pillar of our society and when this system collapses or simply changes, it is an entire society and the future of a country that is falling apart.

How a society chooses to educate its children will inevitably have consequences on their future and the nation's. Indeed, the way of thinking of an individual will develop upon the teachings they receive. King Salomon underlines this aspect: "Raise up a child in the way it should go! When he grows old, he will not depart from it". (Proverbs 22:6). The brands, advertising companies and other groups also understand this principle very well. They know that the future of a society builds up with the children of today. It is no longer surprising to see some groups attempt to impose their point of view on the educational system. This explains why, lately, the so-called educational networks have been wanting to teach the theory of gender in school.

Some European countries have already started. Parents have no other choice but to be vigilant and monitor the education provided to their children.

d) The government and laws

Citizens trust their political leaders less and less. There are multiple reasons for this, one being that they are proving less and less capable of finding solutions to the issues encountered by the nationals: unemployment, insecurity, the cost of living, etc. The second cause is their personal lack of exemplarity highlighted every day by the media.

After leaving Egypt, Moses found himself alone at the head of a large people. He asked the people to choose among themselves some wise and intelligent men known by all, so that they would help him lead the people. He told them:

> But how can I bear your problems and your burdens and your disputes all by myself? Choose some wise, understanding and respected men from each of your tribes, and I will set them over you. (Deuteronomy 1:12)

These are some of the criteria that every political leader, every senior person should demonstrate so the citizens regain trust in those who govern them. They need upright, honest, intelligent people, who prioritize the country's interests before their own.

The Bible tells us the story of a young man named Daniel, to whom God gave, as well as to his three companions "knowledge and understanding of all kinds of literature and learning." (Daniel 1:17). He worked within the Royal Court and the King said of him that he was ten times above others, in terms of intelligence and wisdom. I think that in such a particular period of time, God wants to raise new Daniels: men and women with a divine wisdom and an intelligence, capable of bringing new solutions, creating new economic and financial systems, reducing the social fracture, bringing social reconciliation among people and communities. God wants to use the government sphere and laws to have people there who could help rebuild the country, with the wisdom that will come from Him and from the Word of God, that contains not only judicial laws but also financial and economic principles. This is what He did with the nation of Israel when they left Egypt. When they arrived in Egypt, they were some 70 persons and when they were about to leave, they were more than two million.

After 430 years of slavery, they had neither laws nor money, nor economic or educational systems. But God gave them laws, commandments, principles concerning family life, life in society, economy, education, justice, etc. In respecting all these principles, the nation, at the time of King David about 300 years later, became one of the most prosperous nations in the world. The Bible says that the fame of Israel was such that the Queen of Saba moved from Ethiopia to meet King Salomon, in order to verify by herself if everything she had heard about this people was true. (Kings 10:7)

e) The media

The sphere of communications and the media are considered as the "fourth power", after the executive, the legislative and the judicial powers. Previously limited to the television, the press and the radio, the media's influence has increased tenfold since the expansion of the Internet.

The Arab Spring of 2011 is a very good example to illustrate the power of the globalization of information and social media. An entire region of the world was outraged by an isolated incident relayed by the media.

On December 17, 2010, a young street vendor burned himself in Sidi Bouzid, a town located in the center of Tunisia, to protest against the seizure of his goods by the police. This led to protests which reached Tunis, the capital. The information was relayed by the media and social networks, and very quickly, the protest against the power in place spread to other neighboring countries like Egypt, Syria, Libya, etc. This was the beginning of what the media called the "Arab Spring". These movements became so significant that some leaders like Ben Ali in Tunisia and Hosni Mubarak in Egypt were forced to leave their position. This shows the influence that media and social networks can have today, especially the Internet. Tools that the Church is using more and more, to connect with believers and unbelievers and deliver its faith and love.

The Internet has become a land without borders, in which all kinds of information and ideologies are circulating and in many cases, without any control. It is very important that Christians take their place on the web, in order to communicate a message and principles that can transform lives and reach people who are not necessarily accustomed to pushing a church door.

f) Arts and leisure

The 21st century is the era of entertainment. Homes are equipped with two, even three televisions, satellite, an Internet box, a computer, a tablet, a smartphone. All these tools give access to a multitude of programs all over the world. A lot of the new habits and customs today seen in society first appeared in TV shows, movies, fashion and have finally been adopted by the overall population.

The people of God must occupy the sphere of arts and recreation, in order to offer other choices and thus make a difference, with TV series that value family and the relationships between parents and children, video clips that respect women, songs with no insults, series that break stereotypes. The people of God must also promote further values, not by imposing them but offering each viewer the possibility of choice. This sphere has an important influence, especially among youngsters, because many are at the stage where they are building their identity, defining their culture and their perception of the world through the music they listen to and the series or films they watch on television.

g) Economy (business, finance, new technologies)

Entrepreneurship is the lifeblood of the economy. Alone, this sector creates the wealth of a country, allows innovation, invents the future, creates employment, determines the quality of life and the influence of a nation. These last fifty years, all Western countries made a major leap in technological advances, that allowed the modernization of their enterprises. Creativity has a lot to do with it.

Very few creators or inventors are aware that many of the ideas they materialize actually come from the Great Creator. Some have noticed, even though they are not believers, that when they give life to an obsessive idea of weeks and even years, something special happens. They feel a very strong intuition, like a 6th sense. For example, Steve Jobs, who through his inventions has propelled the world into a new technological era, confessed that he gave a lot of importance to his intuition and his imagination to create new things. He said:

> Creativity is just the connection of things. When you ask creative people how they made things, they feel a little guilty because they consider they have not done much. They just made real what was in their imagination.

The Holy Spirit wants to stimulate new ideas, new concepts to His people. He wants to give them dreams and divine inspirations so that they create companies, brands, styles, inventions that would change society in making it better. He wants to rise up new leaders, motivated not by amassing profits but concerned about human beings. Many have already started to work. A few months ago, a friend was organizing a business meeting with some twenty entrepreneurs and future entrepreneurs. Among them, web designers, webmasters, cartoon designers, photographers, musicians, videographers, people who work in the audio-visual field. They were all committed to creating and promoting film, web and musical projects addressing other topics than what is seen on television today (sex, drugs, alcohol). In fact, these recurring topics eventually end up influencing society by imposing the point of view of a minority to the majority, and facilitate the spread of minor trends at first, to a larger audience. Whether we like it or not, society and children are ultimately the reflection of what influences us on a daily basis.

3 – The importance for everyone of being well positioned

A Philharmonic orchestra can include up to 100 musicians. To give a performance, each player must first train on their own, in order to become familiar with the musical score, then when all master the part they should play, they can start collective rehearsals.

For the music piece to be played harmoniously, it is important that everyone follows their part, listens to others, knows how to position rightly and respect the rhythm and directions imposed by the conductor. The beauty of the piece lies in the fact that each musician respects their part and follows the conductor. The Great conductor is ready. Holding his wand, he positions the musicians and provides each with the part they will have to play. Everyone is welcome: the single mother, the taxi driver, the plumber, the economist, the maths teacher, the musician, the student, the pensioner, the entrepreneur, the baker, the writer, the storekeeper. Each has a part to play and the part of each is essential for the melody to be beautiful and glorious, so it reflects the magnificence of God.

Some are called to work for "local" spheres (family, groups of friends, sports clubs, etc.), while others are called to work at a national level or even worldwide and to influence large numbers of people. Whatever your sphere, there is no small or large sphere. They all are important in God's eyes. He has placed you there to be a leader, a liberator, a bearer and ambassador of hope, an answer, a solution, a blessing for those who are around you.

Conclusion

Considering the keys which you have just been given in order to discover the purpose of your life and accomplish your destiny, it is now your duty to build a lifetime of success with God. But what is a successful life?

John Wooden gives a wise definition of success: "become the best that you are capable of becoming". The interpretation of this sentence varies depending on the perspective everyone has of life, whether earthly or eternal.

An earthly perspective will lead you to look at earthly successes and personal victories achieved thanks to your own strengths and capacities. In this case, your perception of success mainly depends on the criteria conditioned by society, but also those you have set personally. Thus, many people build their lives and ideals on what society shows them as criteria of success and happiness, simply because the meaning of the word "success" has been overused. This definition gives you no guarantee of having been successful in your life in the eyes of God, even though you might have in people's eyes. There lies the whole problem, as the Bible says: "What good is it for someone to gain the whole world, yet forfeit their soul?" (Mark 8:36).

An eternal perspective requires you to turn your eyes towards the Creator because you know that your success resides in Him. By allowing God to work in your life, you discover His will and in doing His will, you become the best person you could have been and in doing so, you are successful.

After the death of Moses, God spoke to Joshua, His successor, and gave him the key to succeed. He told him:

> Keep this Book of the Law always on your lips; meditate on it day and night, so that you may be careful to do everything written in it. Then you will be prosperous and successful. (Joshua 1: 8)

Today, in addition to the Word of God, the son and daughters of God have the Holy Spirit inside them that leads, teaches, advises, gives them the wisdom and intelligence to fulfill the will of God, and by doing so they become successful in everything they do.

One day, we will all have to appear before the Creator. He then will throw our works into the fire and only those carried out in accordance with His will will last. Until appearing before Him, the only way that enables you to determine whether you have lived your life properly depends on a single question: "Have I done the will of God?"

To answer this question, we must look at Jesus who, in the dawn of His life, was able to tell the Father: "[Father] I have glorified you on earth, I have finished the work you have given me to do." (John 17:4). Will you be able to make the same statement? Your answer, whether positive or negative will enlighten you and tell you whether you are on the right track or if you need to readjust your walk. Your success does not only depend on the Holy Spirit but it also depends on you because, as written in the book of Job: "What you decide on will be done, and light will shine on your ways." (Job 22:28).

To conclude, I would like to offer my own definition of success: **success consists in living each day understanding that the will of God for your life is what is best for you**. This understanding leads you to realize that the best path to a successful life is to write the story God has prepared for you. Your story, added to that of other sons and daughters of God, will have such influence that it will overthrow the criteria of success established by society and align with those established by God. This does not guarantee a long quiet river but by allowing the light within you to shine, you will make God visible to the world and therein your success will reside. Society likes to call "stars" people who have achieved success in one way or another. They shine at the peak of their career, then fade away and people forget them. But this is what God says about His stars, His sons and daughters:

> Those who are wise will shine like the brightness of the heavens, and those who lead many to righteousness, like the stars for ever and ever. (Daniel 12:3)

Thanks

I first want to thank Whitney Jean-Gilles, my business partner and right-hand woman on this project for her corrections, her excellent ideas and dedication.

I express all my gratitude to Katayi Tshinsele, Laetitia Benoit, Melody Smit, Lemaine Bazile, Wilfried Idiatha and Thierry Grappotte for the relevance of their reviews and feedback; not to mention the expertise of Ulrich AK.

My thanks to pastors Jean Bertil and Nadia Ngola, to pastor Franck Lefillatre and to Benjamin Derand.

Great thanks to Alex Richards and Marie Verpilleux for the translation.

Thanks also to all those who, like me, believe that we are at a time when the sons of God must be made manifest: Philippe Dulac, Pascal Itoua, Kanda Kabangu, Max Nagels and Zy Yeung.

Thanks to the Group of young people (you will recognize yourselves) for your thirst for learning and understanding the Word of God. This project was born thanks to you.

Finally, I thank the whole "Prayer projects" team, Kelly, Maïté, Scott, Sally, Aline, Kayser, Magali, Sandrine, Jimmy and Patricia.

Table of contents

Introduction 11

FIRST PART
The consequences of a world without God 15

    Chapter 1
    The thought of God from
    Antiquity to our days 17

    Chapter 2
    The modern world in crisis? 27

SECOND PART
Between God and Man 39

    Chapter 1
    The first men and the redemption plan for humanity 41

    Chapter 2
    A new spiritual beginning 67

    Chapter 3
    Between the Holy Spirit and Man 75

THIRD PART
Begin living a victorious life 95

    Chapter 1
    Be released from the past 97

    Chapter 2
    From the trial by fire to victory 109

FOURTH PART
Destiny 127

    Chapter 1
    From victory to destiny 129

    Chapter 2
    D.E.S.T.I.N.Y 149

    Chapter 3
    Discover your destiny 161

    Chapter 4
    Your gifts and talents 195

    Chapter 5
    Destined to change the world 209

Conclusion 233

Thanks 237

www.ingramcontent.com/pod-product-compliance
Lightning Source LLC
Chambersburg PA
CBHW020850090426
42736CB00008B/318